ACTIVE
FOOTSTEPS

This is a volume
in the Arno Press Collection

SIGNAL LIVES
Autobiographies
of American Women

Advisory Editors

Annette Baxter
Leon Stein
Barbara Welter

See last page of this volume
for a complete list of titles.

ACTIVE FOOTSTEPS

CAROLINE NICHOLS CHURCHILL

ARNO PRESS

A New York Times Company
New York • 1980

920.72
S 578

Editorial Supervision: RITA LAWN

Reprint Edition 1980 by Arno Press Inc.

Reprinted from a copy in The Wisconsin State Historical Society Library

SIGNAL LIVES: Autobiographies of American Women
ISBN for complete set: 0-405-12815-0
See last page of this volume for titles.

Manufactured in the United States of America

Library of Congress Cataloging in Publication Data

Churchill, Caroline M   Nichols, 1833-
    Active footsteps.

    (Signal lives)
    Reprint of the 1909 ed. published by the author,
Colorado Springs.
    1. Churchill, Caroline M. Nichols, 1833-
2. Feminists. United States--Biography. I. Title.
II. Series.
HQ1413.C48A32 1980   305.4'2'0924   [B]   79-8781
ISBN 0-405-12830-4

203089

ACTIVE
FOOTSTEPS

CAROLINE NICHOLS CHURCHILL
At Forty Years.

ACTIVE FOOTSTEPS

BY

CAROLINE NICHOLS CHURCHILL

Author of

"Little Sheaves," "Over the Purple Hills,"
"Class Legislation," Etc.

AND

Editor and Proprietor of

"The Antelope," a Monthly Published Three Years,
and "The Queen Bee," Established 1879, Devoted to the Interests of Humanity,
Woman's Political Equality
and Individuality.

COLORADO SPRINGS
MRS. C N. CHURCHILL, Publisher
1909

Dedication

TO THE RAILROAD MEN OF THE WEST
THIS LITTLE VOLUME IS DEDICATED BY THE AUTHOR,
A FRIEND OF THE WORKINGMEN
THE WORLD OVER.

interest of their own sex. Learn what it means to be constantly coached in the interests of a dominant class. Women of sense will not become the tools of the vicious, but a fool can be coached without knowing the object of the schemer.

If men had to do their vile work without the assistance of woman and the stimulant of strong drink they would be obliged to be more divine and less brutal. The question of the servant girl would be three-fourths settled if woman would give the servant the protection to which even the nurse girl is entitled. Slavery of any character is a most pitiable condition: that of woman keeps the entire race at a low standard. Man has done more for humanity in the last hundred years, since woman began to have influence from the fact of being educated, than has been accomplished in two thousand years previously. The race would be vastly benefited if women were better protected in their enterprises, as she is the unselfish dispenser of all earthly gifts to the race; and, with her advancement in educational matters, man is bound to produce a civilization embracing the brotherhood of the entire race, which will result in causing the wants of one the care of all. May the unseen forces speed the day when man shall not be an unmitigated falsifier that he may live by wronging his fellows. This is an epitome of the earnest prayer of every mother living who has sufficient spirituality to make a prayer.

The author of this work has been obliged to do a traveling business for half a century, because of the physical necessity of being as much as possible in the open air. The work has been made doubly hard from the fact that women have no legal protection when in a strange community, and because women are so easily influenced to help in her degradation. The feminine sex are improving in this respect, beginning to see the necessity of defending their own. Woman in a strange community is supposed to be guilty until proved innocent, while man is supposed to be innocent until proven guilty. That a woman's virtue must depend upon her having a chaperone is too absurd for contemplation. The work performed by nuns may be accomplished in the presence of a tag, but man or woman who has anything to do in the way of legitimate business must give undivided attention to the same for success. I kept a record of my whereabouts for twelve years before establishing a paper in Denver; in case there should be malicious talk from responsible parties a rational defense might be made. Crows are liable to fly over anyone's head, with crow talk. The only remedy for this is to kill the crows. Unless the crops are in danger a crow is not worth killing.

CONTENTS.

ACTIVE FOOTSTEPS

ACTIVE FOOTSTEPS

CHAPTER I.

Mrs. Caroline Nichols Churchill was born in the township of Pickering, Upper Province of Canada, December 23, 1833.

Her parents were originally from the United States of America. Her father, Barbour Nichols, served in the United States in the War of 1812, and was honorably discharged on the borders of Canada about the time Tecumseh the Shawnese chief was killed. Her father met and married his first wife in Canada. This resulted in a residence of forty years in a foreign country. Mrs. Churchill's mother was the second wife, and from a family of wealthy Pennsylvania farmers of Holland and German stock. The father having served as a soldier in the war of the Revolution, Mrs. Churchill remembers well the maternal grandmother as a pensioner for her husband's services in the war which brought independence to this country. Mrs. Churchill also knew her father to have a pension for his services in the

War of 1812. The Holland and German stock were the people of strong purpose and eternal diligence; the father stock were intellectual. His father was a naval officer; had his commission from George the Third. He came to help subdue the rebellion against the mother country, and, with his wife, settled in Rhode Island. Mrs. Churchill's father was born in Providence, R. I., 1785. Died 1885. Lived a hundred years.

There are people who would like to know how Mrs. Churchill spent her childhood days. By helping to do everything she was able to do where there is a large family with moderate means.

All families, unless very wealthy, are reared on the socialistic plan: Every individual must contribute to his or her share of care, work and responsibility as soon as old enough. It is the only way the great mass of the human family can be reared. Mrs. Churchill's mother was the second wife of an elderly man, her father being nearly fifty years of age when she was born. The children of this match were generally gifted, but not vigorous physically. In writing of what will seem a long time ago, it must be remembered that Andrew Jackson was serving his second term as President of the United States the year of Mrs.

14

Churchill's birth. The nation was comparatively young, poor and ignorant. There were not the opportunities for education or the acquisition of wealth that now exists. Mrs. Churchill and sisters were called upon to help weed garden, to drop corn, to make and mend family clothing—no small matter before the sewing machine appeared. Elias Howe's sewing machine first appeared in 1841, but many years elapsed before the invention came into general use. The family stocking yarn was spun at home in those days, and the knitting of socks and stockings was no small job for a good old-fashioned family. In the early forties the manufacturers began to buy up the wool, so that women and girls had more leisure. The pastime of this particular family was reading the New York Ledger, the Herald, and Tribune, and any religious paper that came to hand. Mrs. Churchill finds it the custom of men with large and expensive families to hie themselves to some remote corner of the earth, that the family may be reared with less expense. Especially does this method occur in age, when great effort is no longer possible. Where the subject of this sketch lived schools were scarce and of not much account. At the age of thirteen Mrs. Churchill was sent to her maternal grandmother in the United States, where she had the benefit of a few months of a good public school, and improved the opportunity, to the astonishment of the home folks. When she returned, at the age of fourteen, weighing seventy-five pounds, was engaged to teach a private school in the neighborhood. The people requested this, and the mother consented, saying, "If she tires of it she can give it up." This school proved more of a success than many things undertaken later in life. The child was a natural reader and a good speller for her years and opportunities. She knew the multiplication table and the four ground rules, with much hesitation. About the best of her accomplishments was the ability to recite a great number of stories verbally, and all the nursery rhymes then procurable, and to sing twenty-five songs and an innumerable number of hymns. The family, the church and the school had only vocalism in those days, as the star of Jenny Lind had just appeared, and had not shone long enough to enlighten the people upon the importance of instrumental music in the family or church and the school. Twenty-five dollars was the compensation for three months' teaching. There were very few appropriate school books for children; everything but spellers seemed to be made for grown people. Mrs. Churchill's pupils, twelve in number, brought anything they had at all suitable for child reading, even to nursery rhymes. Dick Whittington, Robinson Crusoe and the story of Blue Beard were the classics for the children of her time and locality. Sometimes the little teacher would get out of sight in the morning and shed a few childish tears, because dreading the responsibility of her daily task. The mother usually appeared upon these scenes with words of encouragement, saying, "You know that you enjoy the school when in session as well as you could possibly enjoy the camp meetings you hold when at play on the intervale, where the timber lands echo your voices so gloriously. You sing as if to the stars in the schoolroom; you certainly ought to be happy if it is noise you enjoy." This little talk usually restored calmness and the necessary vim to face another day's work. The young people heard more sermons than anything else, consequently were greatly given to singing, preaching and praying. Holding funeral services was a favorite pastime. This seemed to partake of the tragic, which is certainly an element of

17

human tastes. At last the end of this school term came. Several of the mothers were present to witness the closing exercises, and expressed themselves well pleased with the progress the children had made. Some one says, "What did you do with the money?" Never troubled about that; teaching the school was her part of the affair; the mother took charge of the financial part of the undertaking, and nothing was thought of it. The children had been drilled with all the energy of which the young teacher was capable. Mother's sitting room was the schoolroom. Mrs. Churchill was congratulated upon the fact that she could board at home, as it was customary for teachers to board around; however tired, entertain the neighborhood evenings, and sleep with the children at night. Things have changed for the betterment of the condition of teachers, and yet there is great chance for improvement. Mrs. Churchill was considered eccentric, as people usually are who have studious habits and some idea of the value of time, caring more for books than for dress or spending time on dress parade. It is said she could never be induced to wear kid gloves, because it took too much of her valuable time to put them on and off. Because of exclusiveness in childhood, she was dubbed "The Lady," which was taken, not as a compliment, but as cruel satire. Mrs. Churchill was married in the early fifties. People did not know what else to do with girls, as there were few avenues of employment for them. A husband was selected, and, however inappropriate, the girl was expected to conform to the condition. Anna Dickenson, a young Quaker woman, of great ability as an orator, appeared about this time,1855, and, with the help of other able orators, succeeded in getting a number of avenues of employment opened to women, and helped create a public sentiment in behalf of the colored slave. Things have been improving ever since for all mankind, as far as sentiment can make for the better. Mrs. Churchill had but eleven or twelve years of married life; her husband died in the early sixties, leaving a young daughter to rear. The young men, pioneers of a new country, were speculating in real estate, and, as panics are created for the purpose of catching the unwary, all were financially ruined. In 1860 the North and South were splitting hairs over technicalities; later they got down to what men call business, what women know to be very poor management. This, how-

In this day and age a woman does not quite belong to others unless she is a society woman or a school teacher. Teachers can be found in many parts of the country dying of tuberculosis, who have been killed by being called upon to entertain the idle, after exhausted with the day's duties. Mrs. Churchill came to the conclusion that a woman with minor children to care for should be a pensioner. Men do not want her as a competitor in business, and it is certainly very unfair to expect her to perform the duties of men without either opportunity or protection. Men certainly make themselves very ridiculous in their worry about race suicide, when no effort of a practical character is ever made whereby thousands might be saved from untimely deaths from unavoidable poverty.

Mrs. Churchill's only living child chanced to be strong and healthy, so that, in some respects, the conditions were not so burdensome as many a poor mother endures. Mrs. Churchill was never in a state of health to take much responsibility in the way of business, especially if the occupation should require indoor labor.

The time came when a married sister could give her daughter a home indefinitely. This gave the mother an opportunity for something in the way of preparing herself for occupations that would at least give a chance for something better than a state of invalidism. California climate was tried. The outdoor life was the only means by which even fair health could be maintained, so canvassing was resorted to for an occupation. The sea did not agree with this case, at the same time the outdoor occupation did for summer employment. When winter came the exposure of travel was abandoned for study in doors. This was the time Mrs. Churchill devoted to getting out her own books—little descriptive works, that pleased the people of that locality, and they sold readily. The Californians are the most generous, genial and hospitable folks to be found in any country. Mrs. Churchill declares there is something in that climate that causes its inhabitants to appreciate the good qualities of others that she has never observed to the same extent elsewhere. Mrs. Churchill was in California from 1870 until 1876. The reason of her change of home was because of finding a climate better suited to her constitutional peculiarities. A high altitude and dry climate made more difference in her whole life than she ever thought possible in any country on earth.

Here is a little personal sketch that may be of interest to some reader of this book. Mrs. Churchill is in height five feet and four inches; bust measure, thirty-two inches; waist, twenty-nine. Rather small hands and feet. Fair skin, with very red lips, but little color in face. Rare white hands. Very brown hair, one of the light nut brown shades, not very abundant; study ever caused it to fall. Eyes an intellectual gray, with drooping lids. Nose rather small, known as a fine nose. Lips full, with strong teeth, rather inclined to be what is known as "out mouthed." Chin large enough for firmness, with genial expression and pleasant smile. Head measures twenty-one and a half inches around, which is average; fourteen and seven-eighths inches from center of ear, which is more than average. Neck, twelve and a half inches. Great animation in countenance when talking. Her chief attraction. Constitution rather light; health seldom perfect. A student by mental temperament. Not mathematical nor mechanical, but an abstract reasoner. Order of brain, statesmanship, philosophical and poetical. Not really great in anything but perseverance, firmness and self-respect. Longs for a more ideal civilization. Is so much in earnest upon this point as to give the best years of her life towards this attainment. Naturally peaceable in disposition. Had the reputation in early life of never striking a brother or sister or a pet of any description, nor forgiving an insult or injury. Later in life, with a larger mental growth, finds no one of sufficient importance to hate. Her self-esteem looks upon the human family as too insignificant, and irresponsible, to even despise. Charity covers the entire race. Temperament, emotional, sympathies easily excited. Has a strong sense of self-preservation. In childhood seldom took risks that children do, in climbing, jumping from high places, and so forth. Was called lazy, and an inveterate old granny, for the above reasons. Was quiet and retiring, preferring books and music to society. Early in life was dubbed "strong minded." Had very little interest in neighborhood topics. Was distinguished for speeches remarkable. Was never popular; there was nothing in it, for this individuality. Had a remarkable musical voice, for strength and sweetness. A memory that few could equal in the way of events of general importance and statistics, but could not remember the component parts of sour milk griddle cakes, until age developed stronger will power.

CHAPTER II.

THE PERILS OF SLEIGH-RIDING.

Mrs. Churchill says she does not care for sleigh-riding, in fact would rather never see snow; she gives an experience which settled this matter with her for all time. Sleigh-riding is ever a fashionable amusement in snowy latitudes. The Upper province of Canada, now known as Ontario, was the scene of this narrative. Cousin Asa was going to Skugog Island on business, and wanted Mrs. Churchill's father to accompany him. The father was not long in discovering that he also had some collecting to do upon the Island. This chanced to be the birth day of the subject of this sketch, her twelfth, and she began to believe herself quite a young lady. The mother interceded in behalf of two of the little girls; as the weather was pleasant there seemed no objection to giving the children an outing, it was so near the Christmas Holidays, December 23rd.

There were friends upon the Island who would be glad to entertain the children for the few hours of their stay. The young folks danced with glee, as the real holiday spirit was abroad, and the thought of a fifteen mile ride in one day, and back the next, was fraught with a world of novelty. The probabilities of a safe journey were thoroughly discussed by the wisdom of the assembly, and the young people dressed out for the occasion in warm, home-spun clothing; there were thick hoods and warm cloaks, and stockings were drawn over the shoes, in place of overshoes. There was little attempt at display on such occasions at any time, and least of all when visiting on this Island of uneuphonious cognomen, as the people were very plain, living mostly by spearing fish through the ice in winter and trapping fur-bearing animals.

The men of the party were thought by the children to be great, kingly-looking fellows, although they now know neither were over five feet five and a half. To the young girls their father and wealthy farmer cousin were the embodiment of all manly virtues, wisdom and greatness. The father was dressed in homespun grey, with an overcoat made of buffalo skins, with collar and cap to match; his leggings were of wool sheep skin. The cousin wore a great coat of grey homespun, with leggings and overshoes that made his legs look like the picture of a polar bear. The horses were big, blooded bays, each wearing a string of bells that could be heard for more than a mile. Robes were in abundance, consisting of homespun kersey blankets woven with a twill, buffalo and bear skin robes, cushions and feather pillows. It was well this party were to remain over night, as the days are short in those latitudes, especially both sides of the holidays. There is not much time for keeping the lamps trimmed for burning to lighten the long evening's work. The young folks were placed in the body of the sleigh, as it was thought they could hold the covering over themselves better than if occupying a seat. The children were full of giggle and cheap wit, the latter being fired unsparingly at the two monarchs on the front seat. One said "they looked like great bears when in reality they were only old dears." The little folks were enthusiastically happy at the turn affairs had taken to give them such an unexpected treat. The main comfort of child life is that they know nothing of the comedies and tragedies of life. The comedy is all they care to see. "Hope springs eternal" or what were the use of trying existence?

As the afternoon advanced it became colder. There were nine miles to be traversed on the open ice before the other side of the Island could be reached. Just before going upon this expanse of ice a wayside inn appeared. This place was either called the "Last Chance" or "The Dew Drop Inn." The children were too unsophisticated to understand the nature of the joking sign, and too cold to ask the usual quota of questions; but for these facts the true name would not at this date have been mixed with doubt. The entire party alighted at the Inn and refreshed themselves, as was customary in the dark old days of whiskey toddies or rum punches. The father of the young girls was a church member in good standing, but in those days the church never meddled with a man's politics unless it should interfere with the minister's salary. In that case it might be *"different."* There was a little jug in the sleigh, holding about a quart, a type of the much sung "Little Brown Jug." This was brought from its hiding and filled with what was understood to be the real "Highland Dew." This narrative will prove that men were the same order of grafters in ye old time as at present. What was consumed in the house at the time, no doubt from the necessities of the occasion, was genuine, as it required much diluting for the younger members of the company. As the well warmed party returned to the sleigh the landlord remarked: "It will be a cold ride away from the sheltering timber." Continued he, "You will be obliged to face the bleak north wind for about nine miles. The ice carries a great deal of snow, and the drive will be slow, try as you will. You cannot reach your destination until dark, and do your best. Look to the little girls often." This was the admonition of one who lived near the lake, and had become weather wise in regard to the location. As soon as the ice was reached a change came over the entire party. The huge horses settled down to hard pulling. The bells were less musical. The giggling of the young folks ceased. The whole party seemed to feel impending trouble, the nature of which could not be remedied by discussion. The sleigh creaked and groaned as it labored through the obstructed road. The ice occasionally cracked with a booming noise, like the distant roar of thunder or booming of cannon. Great crevices appeared in the icy road, which the horses evidently understood, as they passed over them without seeming to notice anything remarkable. The children were afterwards told that the fishes could not live in the waters of these small lakes but for those great cracks in the ice, which brought them fresh air. Occasionally the young folks peeped out enough to see the fishermen's huts upon the ice, where they were sheltered while taking the big salmon trout and other fishes. The horses had changed color so that their own groom would scarcely have known them. From handsome bays they had become as white as the beard of Santa Claus. The hard pulling had made them sweat; the frost had done the rest. The faithful creatures snorted frequently to keep their nostrils free from ice. The two monarchs on the driver's seat resembled polar bears more than ever, their headgear being more or less covered with frost, and something like anchor ice.

The father turned frequently to the little girls, evidently with anxiety, wishing mentally, without doubt, that they had remained at home. Mattie, the younger child, was of a very active temperament, and did her best to make things lively. When about half the distance had been gone over the lake, she shouted as if the necessity were a very urgent one: "Father and Cousin Asa, is it not time to try the little brown jug? I am cold and need something to warm me up." The father passed the little jug, saying as he did so, "Get the cork out if you can." Mattie was equal to the occasion, but quickly returned it, saying, "It is frozen up." The jug was returned to its former resting place with a frozen bounce. The quality of that "Mountain Dew" was said to be "strained." The father remarked that there was little danger of this branch of the family freezing to death, but the other child would lie there and perish without demonstration.

At length the journey came to an end. The destination was reached. Mattie was first out of the sleigh to announce the coming of the others. The subject of this sketch was found to be unconscious, and with much anxiety carried into the house. When she regained her senses a large open fire-place with a well constructed wood fire was the first thing that met her gaze. Her hands and feet were undergoing manipulation. "She is not frozen," said the father, "only chilled," but ten minutes more might have finished her career."

Next day home was reached without unpleasant experiences, as the ride was in the forenoon.

Mrs. Churchill has never since been partial to snow or ice, or sleigh-riding.

The temperance people who read this sketch can take heart at the way they have changed public sentiment in the last half century. Mrs. Churchill is not one who thinks reforms come without effort or agitation. The very sentiment against strong drinks was brought about by persistent effort on the part of intelligent women and the churches they represent. There has been accomplished in the last hundred years more for humanity and more in discovery and invention than was brought about in two thousand years of entire man management. Within a hundred years woman's education has created an influence that no half-civilized nation has experienced. Note the difference! The wisest of men begin to think that no nation can long continue in development of its greatest achievements or possibilities without the councils of a womanhood of sufficient influence to help mould national affairs. There are now influences at work to belittle the masses of mankind and keep them for drudges. But if woman continues in mental development there will be found a remedy for most of the serious social ills that exist. We are living out the adage all have heard reiterated so many times, that two heads are better than one if one is a woman's.

CHAPTER III.

It was the latter part of August, 1862. The Governor of the state sent word to the people that it were better in some localities for the inhabitants to leave the country for a time at least, as it would be impossible to give them protection in their own homes. Mrs. Churchill was teaching in a country place, but near a post office, where the possibility of getting the latest intelligence was much better than in most localities. One beautiful hazy day in August a band of Indians came in sight of the schoolhouse, dismounted from their ponies, placing their guns across the back of their steeds and began firing. Although they were quite a distance from the house, the children could not be detained. The grass over a greater part of the country was yet wild and tall. In two minutes there was not a child in sight. Mrs. Churchill concluded that she would hold the fort by hiding behind the open door, as this gave the room the appearance of having been vacated. The teacher hardly be-

35

lieved that an attack would be made this time of day, as the harvest was going on and there were many persons in the fields that could have been assembled for defense against so small a band. Next day, however, eight families had concluded to vacate. The pigs were let out of their pens, the canary birds were set free, the horses were harnessed to all manner of vehicles and the cattle were driven as an asset, as money was very scarce in a community of pioneers. It was difficult to make any progress through several days' journey, because of the great anxiety of the people living along the road to get the latest information from the seat of war. The train was constantly stopping, until the men became accustomed to the situation and learned to manage by cutting the questioners very short. All kinds of rumors were afloat. It would seem that frightening women with unnecessary fiction was a part of Indian warfare.

The first night out was spent in a house deserted the day before, for the same reason that others were left. For the first few days those starting from the same neighborhood remained together. Some had friends they could tarry with until something definite could be determined upon.

Mrs. Churchill's party was bound for Winona, Minn. The first night out there was a larger number to be fed and sheltered than at any time during the trip. Mrs. Churchill was the most mature woman in the caravan who had no young children to care for, nor any one specially to look after when tired out from cattle driving, so took it upon herself to superintend what was needing general supervision. Clean straw was brought from lately-threshed stacks and an abundance of it put upon the upper and the lower floors of the house; as there were only two rooms, both of goodly proportions, the carpeting was easily accomplished. The women took entire charge of the upper floor, while the men occupied the entire lower part. In making arrangements for supper the women did themselves credit by getting up a lug pole that would hold two great kettles that had been used for rendering lard. Then a fire like a small log heap made it possible for every one to get an ear of boiled corn and potatoes for their need. These necessities were foraged from an immense field adjoining the house. Everybody who had anything to say remarked, "that if the people were at home we would pay for this; but as they are not, we will forage, as it is war time!"

of the women who knew what a child means to a mother attempted the pig paths until they found themselves as liable to get lost in the approaching darkness and tall grass as the child. The mother was prevailed upon to retire, as fretting would only endanger the infant in her arms. The theory was accepted that the child had fallen asleep, as no child of five years would be liable to remain long awake after his bed time and such an exciting day's experience. The young boys had discovered wild plums in abundance and had gone forth in great anticipation, the little one as enthusiastic as any, but when the children were ready to return to green corn and potatoes the youngest had gone from sight and did not answer to the calling of the others. Mrs. Churchill had noticed some fattening hogs that had been turned loose the day before. These creatures were amusing themselves tearing at the stacks of newly harvested grain, running and snorting as if ready for any vicious fun. Mrs. Churchill says she would have been afraid to encounter one of them. It occurred to her that these swine would be the most dangerous things that could come to the exhausted child. No one else seemed to have thought of this, so there was nothing said about the matter.

of his wanderings, or of his fears, but this much is certain, he made great effort, as the man in charge of the cornfields said it was certainly nine o'clock when he retired and he was quite sure the child was not upon the door step at that time.

The saddest story of this retreating campaign has yet to be told. Several mothers lost their youngest children from cholera-infantum. The hardships were too much for the little ones to bear and live. There was a very interesting little girl of three years in the family with whom Mrs. Churchill made her home while teaching the school so rudely broken up. The stork came very late in life to the old people who were the parents of this dear little girl; the father over sixty, the mother forty-six years of age. Children are seldom more welcome than was little Cora. With a lovely disposition, she was rollickingly funny in her amusements, with a wonderful gift of mimicry. When engaged in anything requiring dignity of deportment, she was not wanting. These people kept the post office for that section, and when there was a call for mail Cora frequently stated to the parties in advance in the most approved manner, calling the parties by name: "Mrs. Jones, there is a letter for you," or "Mr. Stewart, you will find papa in the field at work." The next youngest in the family was a sister of sixteen. Cora began the day with a romping play, usually with this big sister. Some one would tell her that it was time sister and school "Marm" were up, as they might be too late for breakfast. Cora had been instructed as to the most effective way of getting people up in the morning. It was to throw a little water upon them. Cora had a gill cup from which she took her draught of new milk. This was before time for her milk, so she started for sister's room, the stair door being opened to give her a fair chance. Sister and the school "Marm" could hear her chuckle of delight as she started out on such an audacious undertaking. By the time the rooms were reached the cup would not have more than half a dozen drops, as most of it had been spilled upon her own "nighty." She chuckled so hard over her scheming that her hand was not at all steady. She made her demand; that sister and school "Marm" get up "or she would souse them." She knew this was child's play, so did her best to make the few drops of water go around, throwing it so at random that seldom a drop took effect.

The child expressed a desire for a nice hat. There were no nice little hats to be had at the pioneer stores. It is likely there would be poor sale for such a class of goods, as in a country so new there were not many places for people to go, and the children could wear sunbonnets and go barefooted. There were none to be had short of Mankato, a town forty miles distant, and no one to send by to get one but some man, and millinery bought under such conditions was not at all likely to be very satisfactory. Mrs. Churchill had learned this business with sewing and straw dressing, as this used to be a part of millinery. One Saturday when there was time the old discarded bonnets were looked up and enough fancy French braid found for the desired hat. No time was lost that day, and before night the headgear was ready to wear, as the braid being a kind of straw lace required only sewing into shape. There was no time lost in bleaching and blocking, as this was not necessary. There was white satin ribbon enough to be found on the place to do the trimming. This little luxury was paraded for the admiration of every member of the family and any chance neighbor. In the child's jocose way, she pronounced the school "Marm" "a pretty nice

43

eral days, as her constitution was an exceptionally strong one, and passed away without wearing her new hat. This young child, but three years of age, was so full of jolly fun, song and dance, laughter and mimicry, everything calculated to enliven the hard lines of human life. She has been missed and mourned for nearly half a century as few of the race are. The dearest sentence in the language to a woman is "My baby."

CHAPTER IV.

WINONA, MINNESOTA.

The Winona people received the refugees kindly. Mrs. Churchill found a home in the family of Warren Powers, elderly people, refined and lovely. Mr. Powers was the nephew of President Millard Fillmore. The President exchanged visits with his nephew during his term of office. Mr. Powers was probate judge when Mrs. Churchill knew him, and showed an appreciation of the coming woman's influence by consulting "the strong minded," as brainy women are sometimes dubbed. There were decisions on the distribution of property in which women were, or should be as much interested as if it were a personal matter of their own. Men of brain and heart have ever realized the abject helplessness of woman when property was to be distributed among different claimants. A class must show themselves fit for something more than serfdom in order to get any recognition of their rights at all. Women have proven what it is possible for them to do within the last fifty years. All women should take heart at what

46

has been done in making man superior to a drunken booby. This chapter shows one thing to be true of which men have accused woman so often, that is, being a sermonizer. Is it any wonder women preach, when for ages the preaching all seemed aimed at her defenseless head? It is the only method of which she is perfectly familiar, and so long as she has been a patient sufferer from man's method of management, he should have the grace to submit when he sees his methods imitated. Mrs. Churchill says he does submit with a fair show of being susceptible of receiving a higher education than the women of sixty years ago would have thought possible. Let us not be discouraged; he belongs to us at any rate, and it is our duty to make something of him if we can, and so long as he has the manhood to forego strong drink there is hope that some day we will have a civilization fit to live in.

Mrs. Churchill ever remembers the people of Winona with a feeling of gratitude for the interest taken, and the appreciation of her own order of abilities. There are only a few who care to see character development. This was not the case with the people of Winona. There were many good intentions shown Mrs. Churchill while she tarried

47

with them by the best class of people. But "there is a destiny that shapes our ends, rough hew them how we may." Mrs. Churchill made a sale of some property about this time, and wishing to have a permanent home for herself, was advised to seek an older and wealthier community to establish her business—millinery and dressmaking. In ability she proved a success, but in a few months found anything requiring so much constant care, housing and close application; health must be sacrificed, and in the end life. Mrs. Churchill always thought that a warmer climate would give her a better chance to do something worth while, as her health improved in warm weather.

The people with whom Mrs. Churchill made her home while in Winona, Minn., had a sister who occasionally spent a winter with her brother, Warren Powers, she being also the niece of President Fillmore, and mother of the Leeland hotel proprietor, who kept the Windsor in New York, that a few years ago was destroyed by fire. Mrs. Leeland at that time was an elderly matron, fine looking, well dressed and when telling short stories with her brother, a man over sixty years of age, they were a very interesting couple. Mr. Powers had some time in early life served as clerk in a grocery store at some point where the Sleepy Hollow, N. Y., people came to trade. His stories gleaned from real life were well worth hearing. It gives a sample of the way many of our ancestors did economize when rearing their families, many of whom may now be leaders in this "great and glorious." (The sample.) Nearly through trading. He: "Mother, how are we fixed for knives and forks?" She: "I think we kin git along a spell yit. There is the butcher nife, shoe nife, pumpkin nife, cob handle and shackle back, Jim's nife without a handle. He don't care."

As the subject of short stories has been mentioned, I will here give some of Mrs. Churchill's. Going from a point on the railroad to Mineral City, Arizona, the transportation is by a local stage. Mrs. Churchill, in praising the well-groomed team, found that the man was not only a driver, but the owner of the outfit, highly intelligent and an ideal worshiper of what we are pleased to term the lower order of animals. In the course of conversation he remarked: "I will show you my three owls about two o'clock this afternoon. Little birds

that await by the wayside every day for my coming." The man had so many commissions to fill in
the way of errands that Mrs. Churchill entirely
forgot about the owls. At length two o'clock came
and the horses halted at a bunch of chaprel. The
man remarked: "There are my owls." Sure enough
there were the three little owls standing in the
most perfect composure, basking in the most un-
heard of confidence and blinking in the bright
sunlight. They were serene, plump and billowy,
as if there were no ruffling of plumage or other
distracting features to disturb the placid life of
young owls in this part of the country. This was
a picture that would have brought an exclama-
tion of surprise and delight from an Audubon.
Owls could never have appeared to a better advantage. "The Owl Man," as Mrs. Churchill has
ever since designated him from the rest of humanity, made the remark that he never cracked his
whip at any animal or creature, nor did he ever
speak harshly to them. Most animals show love,
appreciation and thankfulness when well treated
by the human lord. This proves beyond doubt that
the lower order of animals well understands
man's superior power over them. If man used

his power generally as a true king should, only destroying what he must in self-defense and not terrorizing any creature, we might enjoy a much happier world.

CHAPTER V.

TRUE SHORT STORIES.

Several years later Mrs. Churchill was crossing the Courthouse square in the city of Los Angeles, Cal., when a well dressed gentleman accosted her by name, asking if she remembered the "Owl Man." "I most assuredly do," said Mrs. Churchill. "Is it possible my eyes again behold the 'Owl Man?'" After a cordial greeting the two seated themselves on a settle and visited fifteen or twenty minutes, giving each their own modern history as transpired since the time of the owl episode. After a little detail of his late trip to China, Mrs. Churchill's sketch of her business enterprises, the mutual admirers parted with good wishes exchanged, each presuming that this would be the final greeting on this terrestrial ball. Four or five years later Mrs. Churchill was ascending one of the hills at Leadville, Colo., when she noticed a citizen riding with the driver of an ore team, coming down the hill. The citizen hailed Mrs. Churchill, calling her name, and with the same interrogation asked if she still remembered the "Owl Man?" "I do," was the response. "Are you the 'Owl Man?'" "I am," was the hurried answer, as the team trotted down the hill and Mrs. Churchill was going up the hill. There was no time for ancient or modern history. With a wave of the hands the two admirers parted, likely never to meet again unless it should be that he chance to read this chapter and take the trouble to come on purpose to see one who admires a man not so much for his occupation as for his fine, manly, kingly traits. Mrs. Churchill does not know that she ever heard this man's name and certainly never expects to see him again, unless in the "Sweet By and By," "where the wicked cease from troubling and the weary are at rest." It would be interesting to know when and how the owls lost confidence in his lordship man. With the next mail carrier, likely. Dear, beautiful owl picture. Mrs. Churchill says she considers this the most lovely incident of her forty years of traveling life.

On a fifth of July Mrs. Churchill was going up one of those long hills in Leadville when accosted by two young boys, eight or nine years of age and so near of a size as to suggest a healthy pair of twins. Both were armed with toy pistols, carried behind, until Mrs. Churchill was confronted with the weapons presented in such a manner as would indicate special training. "Halt!" came in concert and one breath from both the youngsters. Again strong evidence of training, Mrs. Churchill halted, of course. This was the correct thing under the circumstances. She could not well hold up her hands without letting her papers fall. She thought it advisable to try the effect of logic on the highwaymen. Said she: "Boys, if I were going to hold up and rob some one I would not take an old gray-haired woman. "Be you an old gray-haired woman?" "Of course, I am," said she. "Do you not see my white hair?" "Yes," said he. "That is different," said the spokesman, each letting his hand with the pistol drop by his thigh. Mrs. Churchill continued her way, rejoicing that real Western highwaymen were so susceptible to feminine logic.

A STORY OF LYDIA THOMPSON'S TIME.

Mrs. Churchill has always sold her books and papers in all business places, regardless of conventional custom, because she knew that those customs were made by a ruling class in the interests of that class, and not in the interests of women.

On one occasion she was going into a saloon with a little book of her own writing, called "Little Sheaves." The owner of the place met her pale and trembling. Said he: "I suppose you have come to pray. "'Not unless you spell it 'prey,'" replied Mrs. Churchill. "I am only a harmless book vender selling my own books." Whereupon a reaction set in and the man bought several copies. Says Mrs. Churchill: "What made you think that I had come to pray with you, when alone. The praying people go in bands." He answered: "You have a very pious complexion."

THE BED SLIPPER.

It was midnight on the day coach of a railroad train. Everybody seemed to be tired out and sleepy. The people were reclining as is wont on such occasions. The train stopped at a station. Two big, well-dressed and well-groomed citizens of the U. S. A. came aboard, who were evidently neighbors when at home, but neither knew of the other's coming. They exchanged greetings, and without a thought of the existing state of things, fell to discussing crops and financial affairs in a loud tone, proving thereby that they had been sleeping several hours and were fresh and vigorous for what business awaited them. No heed was paid to sundry groans and sleepy grunts. Mrs. Churchill, never a vigorous person, was greatly disturbed and made up her mind that for the common defense, something must be done. She aroused, loaded with wrappings, pulled a little bed slipper from her hand baggage, shook it at the men as they were near the entrance, where a good view could be had of the nature of the weapon. Said she: "Gentlemen, do you see this?" They had been correctly addressed, for not another whisper was heard from that source during the rest of the night. A suppressed titter from some indiscreet one in the back of the car was the only visible demonstration.

THE RESTING OXEN.

In Houston, Texas, Mrs. Churchill was out attending to the sale of her book. It had rained the night before and the streets were in a bad condition for teamsters. There came along a big load of lumber, drawn by several yoke of oxen. Mrs. Churchill says she never saw as many teams succeeding one another as there were in this outfit. The driver was an intelligent looking negro with as fine a set of teeth as one will ever see in any man's head. One of the leaders of this long team had laid down, evidently completely tired out; the rest of the oxen began to follow the example of the leader. Houston was a pretty busy city to have a street obstructed in this way any length of time. But the driver sat grinning, evidently enjoying the situation as those people usually do. There was no slashing of the whip, no profanity to demonstrate hereditary piety; just waiting for something to turn up or for the oxen to get up when wanting a change of position. Mrs. Churchill came and asked the teamster how far he had driven that long team through the muddy roads. He gave a polite answer and the conversation led to asking why he did not give his team more rest. Said he, with a very broad smile: "I think they is a restin', Miss."

RACE CHARACTERISTICS.

Mrs. Churchill noticed that in addressing any of the brunette races she always received civil answers, which is not so liable to be the case with the white people. There is a strain of affability, politeness and geniality that the pale face with a more urgent climate has had less time to consider. A high type of a Southern gentleman cannot be surpassed on earth for fine traits, and their women make the best stepmothers and the best fostermothers that the world produces. Mrs. Churchill's experience with those women verifies this statement. These things others have observed and commented upon.

THE HARNESSED DOG.

At a station in the Indian Territory a boy, ten or twelve years of age, had a big black, shaggy dog harnessed in a little four-wheeled wagon. The day was very warm. The dog's tongue was lolling and he had every appearance of having been worked long enough for once. Mrs. Churchill said: "Brother have you not had the harness on the dog long enough for once? Take him home and let him rest, then you can harness him in the cool of the evening." The boy answered: "Whose dog is this?" Mrs. Churchill knew the type and answered accordingly. Said she: "Don't you know that I own all the dogs in the world and all the boys, too?" She further commanded him to take the harness off the dog and put it on himself and draw that wagon home. The fellow showed fright, as well as astonishment. To say the least, he thought here was a person dangerously erratic. He took that harness off in the greatest possible haste and placed it in the wagon; then in the shafts he started out as fast as he could go with the dog alongside, expressing his pleasure at release from compulsory toil on such a warm day. The boy kept looking back to prove that he was getting out of danger until he was lost to sight in a body of heavy timber through which the road ran. Boys frequently do the best they know when in charge of animals, but lack judgment nearly equal to that of parents who are careless about trusting children too far with the control of animals.

And now we say: "Man born of woman his days are short and filled with crookedness."

CHAPTER VI.

THE FARCE TRIAL.

There is a town or city as may be in the United States that is situated geographically much as the Siamese Twins were physically. This town has two sets of hungry local officials belonging in two different states and having but one spine to separate them; that is the state line. Those states are Texas and Arkansas. Hence, a compound name Texarkana. Mrs. Churchill once came to this place in the regular course of business, when the only way a woman could conduct a traveling business was by constantly having recourse to a retreating campaign. Rest on firearms at night and be ready for an unheralded victory or death any moment. Ever ready for flight, when positive battle was no longer preventible, Mrs. Churchill was selling her own book, entitled "Over the Purple Hills" in one wing of this compound city, an individual without warrant arrested her; it being in one of the Courthouse buildings, there was a fine opportunity for a farce trial. Mrs. Churchill had been informed by good authority that one

could sell their own production anywhere in the
United States of America without paying license.
The District Attorney bore upon his face the imprint of the state of Kentucky and was a very
good-looking specimen of the blue grass Democ-
racy. He with his comrades mourned that it was
so long between drinks. Alas! Their toes peeped
through their shoes, were in local parlance of
the alligator mouth pattern, because of the stitch-
adhering where the leather had worn away.
Their coats had been bleached by the suns of
more than one summer and the storms of more
than one winter. There were several parties of
about the same ilk who were short on business,
but long on time, not knowing where the next
amusement was coming from. "A woman was in
town getting money out of the community, selling
her own book, where we have been getting ragged."
"Women have ever paid us tribute for appearing
on earth at all, and why not call this one down?"
"It will give a little variety to our monotony and
perhaps enough money to 'liquidate' the crowd."
The plan was set in motion, the city officials from
both sides of the state line making a great display of books and documents. Mrs. Churchill had
read of the Ragged Opera being played in Lon-

province. This had a surprising effect. Finally, hungry and tired, she offered them five dollars with which to treat the crowd if the court would adjourn long enough to get supper. The Blue Grass Democrat then told her that she was dismissed, and further remarked: "That she had conducted herself like a lady." She answered: "I wish I could give you men the same compliment; that you had been conducting yourselves like gentlemen. Now if each of you men personating an officer will buy a copy of my book and thus compensate me for the loss of time in being detained forcibly in this farce court I will call it square. Said the District Attorney: "We would do that and be glad to, but there is not five dollars in the crowd. You sized us up correctly in every particular, only we are not so villainous as you think us, and we will prove it by declining the five you offered us as a bribe to adjourn court until you had your supper." When Mrs. Churchill reached her boarding house most of the people had eaten. "Dear me!" said Aunty D, why so late?" An explanation of the affair was given, including the jail threat and the international treaty threat. Aunty was once a practical slave holder and knew how to treat any

CAROLINE NICHOLS CHURCHILL
At Seventy-Six Years.

CHAPTER VII.

The Grass Valley Boarding House.

The boarding house mistress was a large, stout Welsh woman of ideas and a goodly share of executive ability. Her husband was a Norman Englishman. Mr. L——— was of rather slender figure, fair, fine, rosy skin, black eyes and black hair, curly in ringlets, which his indulgent wife kept about his neck for over thirty years. This, too, in democratic U. S. A., where public opinion is both parliament and king. This man and wife, like the Heavenly Twins, contradicted the general idea in regard to the appearance of man and wife. They filled the appearance of Jack Sprat and his wife. Jack Sprat could eat no fat, his wife could eat no lean; so between them both they cleared the cloth and left the platter clean. These people had a handsome residence situated upon a hill which overlooked a good part of the town of Grass Valley. Mrs. Churchill was selling her own book, a little work called "Little Sheaves," and making her sojourn with a family from a Southern State, fine, elderly people. The

L.'s had heard of Mrs. Churchill as a promising young woman of studious habits, aggressive in reform ideas; in fact, a woman inclined to stout shoes and short hair, besides having a fad for sawing off three sticks of wood before breakfast. A woman who seemed unconsciously to violate conventional customs with a reckless disregard of consequences. A person combining so much that was considered eccentric by the "Pin Heads" of society, the L.'s were anxious to see, so invited her to a Sunday dinner when the outlay was unusually elaborate. Mrs. Churchill accepted and found a guest who had taken Sunday dinner with this family for seven years. Certainly a nice custom where people are sufficiently settled in their ways of living to receive their friends with such regularity. The guest was a retired sea captain, a pretty fair story teller, and as his stories were short and true, they never lacked interest. Mrs. Churchill sometimes gets so interested in the upper thought that she loses her bearing—is a poor navigator. Some one smiles and says, "We saw you go by; thought as it was dinner hour, you would come in." Captain says, "Tell them that a pig is the best known navigator."

When a captain at sea loses his bearings he puts a pig overboard, if he has one on board, and the commercial craft usually have. The pig will swim around the vessel until he finds that he cannot get aboard; will then strike out for the shore, and any craft is safe to followin the direction indicated by the pig. But what of the poor beast? A boat is lowered and he is brought aboard before a shark gets him, if possible.

Mrs. Churchill found the L.'s good substantial people, who were more than the average appreciative of the gifts of others. They had no children, and had educated themselves in modern languages, mathematics and bookkeeping after they were married. Mrs. L. remarked to Mrs. Churchill that the interior hotels of California were not the best places in the world to regain lost flesh and retain it. Mrs. Churchill was in miserable health, had a bad cough and did not think herself of getting through another spring time. The L.'s said, "Stay with us, we can feed you up and make you well; we have seen people before who had been starved to ill health when doing a traveling business in the interior of this State." Spanish beef from wild cattle makes very cheap but wretchedly poor meat. Then succession potatoes, grown year after year without cultivation, makes a very coarse tuber, depositing little starch or sugar, but running to fibrous tissue until the American nation would hardly recognize the root of their national greatness without a verbal introduction. The side dish was green beans, canned before the railroad reached the country, and kept because there was no local market and of course no shipping, otherwise they would have been obliged to go around the Horn or across the plains; thus one can plainly see that those beans were tough. The French bread and butter were always good, or starvation outright would have been inevitable. The coffee and tea were wretched; in fact, nothing but the bills were first class. This was thirty years ago or it would not be related here; out of pure national pride the story would be suppressed. That class of landlords have all gone to give an account of their stewardship for the deeds done in the body—things are very different now in that country. This narrative is given more in sorrow than in anger, remembering that those people on the interior felt so keenly their isolation from their former homes that they were ready to sacrifice any other human creature in

the interest of covetousness. The appearance of
the railroad has changed this petty rascality,
from which there was no appeal, to a more respectable order on a larger scale from which
there is also no appeal (it is generally thought
short of), well, revolution, or selling our
eggs by weight instead of count. Mrs. L. continued, "The people of the U. S. A. are poor
dietists, many of them starve to death from
poor cooking, or not knowing how to eat with
best results after cooking is well done." Mrs.
Churchill said, "Those elderly people I am stopping with are so kind and good I do not like to
make a change; I do all their family writing;
neither of them write, although both read, and
are people of more than ordinary intelligence and
information. Whatever our unbelief, it does
seem at times that a destiny shapes our ends."
It began to rain with the inconsistency of dry
climates and gave almost a steady downpour
for a whole week. Mrs. Churchill was very sensitive to dampness, so consented to have some
flannel garments sent for, which in time resulted
in having her entire effects removed to the L.
residence for the rest of the winter, with the
promise that she would see the elderly friends

or a loose joint in the line fence. The civilized man looks upon the necessity of fuel for his family as being an imperative necessity, as much as flour, meat and sugar. If he burns wood, his wood pile is a model, with ever ready kindling to match. This was the case with the L.'s. Mrs. Churchill thought there was no hope for her favorite exercise. This, however, had been talked over by the contracting parties. Mr. L. had promised "the dear old people" that a new woodpile should be created out of whole tree limbs, and the bucksaw put in prime condition, so that Mrs. Churchill should lose nothing by the change of boarding houses, but gain the flesh nature intended she should wear. All this was done and much more; soon as the rains had sufficiently abated the wood sawing went on as usual; first a few sticks answered for a hearty breathing spell, then came the call to breakfast, two tablespoonsful of native grape juice, a small cup of coffee, a poached egg and a couple of slices of dry toast. The dinner came not until four o'clock; the details are given here because of the results that some other person needing to be rescued from perishing in a similar manner might be restored to health by adopting similar methods. In

71

seven months she left the L.'s weighing a hundred and fifty-five pounds, the heaviest she had ever weighed in her life, her weight usually being about one hundred and twenty-five pounds. She weighed but a hundred and fifteen when she first went to the L.'s. At first the time from breakfast to dinner seemed unbearable; the hostess was inexorable, however, had seen similar cases. Mrs. Churchill provided her money for the rainy season during the summer months, so that her winter work might be limited to dry conditions. Thus a pretty good fast could be endured until one became accustomed to the change without danger of collapse. Mrs. Churchill asked for just one cracker to silence the demands of former habit; the request was not granted, the hostess remarking that she, the patient, had come to her to be cured and must submit to discipline if she expected results. Reading and writing were almost entirely prohibited. Dear me! to sit on the front porch under the vines watching the linnets flitting back and forth wondering what they could possibly find to keep them so unremittingly busy—there seemed to be hundreds of them in those vines. This variety of the linnet is very little larger than a big strawberry, and a tiny white feather on its red breast makes it look like an over-ripe strawberry. The week day dinner came at last, and with it a good appetite. There were the best of potatoes, the French leek, one of the onion family cooked as greens, roast beef, and plain boiled suet pudding served with a well made sauce. This suet pudding is said by some to be the real source of English physical greatness—boiling takes starch out of the flour leaving more valuable qualities. It is a pity that the suet pudding is not revived by the housewives of the U. S. A. The Sunday dinner was the main feature of these seven months of life's history. United States fashion, it might be called an "institution." Mrs. L. had made eight English plum puddings late in the fall, each about the size of a human head. They were all cooked at once in a large wash boiler, bought and kept on purpose for extraordinary occasions. Each was covered with tight linen bagging and boiled for four hours without ceasing for one moment. These puddings were made a little plainer than the original recipe. One was given to a friend, the others were put in a cool place for winter use. Mrs. L. evidently understood her business, getting people well from illness caused by hotel or

down to dinner. Two beautiful tortoise shell cats, the three-colored feline of the females, were called and told to get up into a little slit window near the dining table; the time of day gave bright sun on the cats and made a very pretty picture. A part of this performance that was most surprising was the readiness with which the felines responded to the request, as cats have so little imagination that they are usually very stupid about comprehending requests. These cats knew all about rewards and punishments of a local character, for never once during Mrs. Churchill's stay were one or either known to desert her post, but sat out the dinner looking at one another and at the guests with the peculiar genial expression of puss when she is contented and sure of her position. There was another greenhouse on this very interesting place; the house being built upon a hillside made several steps necessary for entrance; these steps ran out well towards the end of a porch making room under the steps for a greenhouse; by putting glass in frames, with a little door mostly glass, it was made a very attractive place—it was filled with the largest variety of pansies one will often see.

On the wall of Mrs. L.'s residence hung a life-size bust picture of the Duchess of Landsfelt, popularly known as "Loly Montez," who was born in Ireland in 1824 and died in New York in 1861. This woman was a celebrated character in the early '50s. She was of Moorish and Irish descent, a great beauty, and withal highly intellectual. An old Bavarian king bestowed the title of duchess upon her, as it saved the troubles arising from a morganatic marriage. "Loly" came to California for the purpose of regaining or making a fortune, was swindled out of the money she had invested, returned to New York, and died in despair in consequence. She was buried in Greenwood cemetery. The marker for her grave bears the simple inscription, "Malinda Gilbert." Her autobiography was in Mrs. L.'s collection of books and was highly appreciated by Mrs. Churchill. "Loly" was a firm anti-Catholic, and gives some strong facts about the workings of that wretched system through Europe. The ignorance of the great mass of the people, consequent lack of preparation to live, crime, beggary and want follow in its wake everywhere. The Duchess of Landsfelt was contemporaneous with Jenny Lind, the great vocalist. Thirty years ago the Grass Valley people could tell amusing stories about "Loly's" pet bear and her wonderful horsemanship. Her horse could clear any of the gates in this little city, with its rider upon its back. The encyclopedia speaks of the duchess as an adventuress. Queer way men have of putting things. I would like to know why the poor Irish emigrant girl, who comes to this country as a domestic servant, is not also designated an adventuress. The master class seldom lose a chance to insult a woman who has the ability for something besides service to his lordship. When women get to be taller in stature than men (which is rapidly coming to pass)—when they write, compile and publish encyclopedias—supposing they set down every man of superior ability and aspiration as an adventurer, a pirate, a thief, a falsifier. How would it sound? Woman will never do that, however tall she grows, because she knows he is hers by discovery. Instead of envying him his ability, she is proud of him.

CHAPTER VIII.

Starting a Paper.

In 1876 Mrs. Churchill went East for the purpose of getting out her little book, entitled "Over the Purple Hills." This work was descriptive of California. It was Centennial year, and it was difficult to get publishers interested in a new book maker, especially one whose reputation as a novice was centered entirely in the "Wild and Fleecy West." Mrs. Churchill had her book printed in Chicago, and reviewed by the "Tribune," the "Times" and "Post." Two of these publications mentioned the book as being a sprightly written little work, with some description surpassing any previous production on those points, "The Yosemite Valley, Lake Tahoe and Monte Diablo." With this she visited Texas, where she traveled for two years, making a generous sale of her work. Missouri, Kansas and Indian Territory assisted in filling the time until 1879. Mrs. Churchill, desiring to make a permanent home for herself, was returning to California, when she visited Denver, Colorado. She had no

men hold in supreme selfishness all the great avenues of influence, the pulpit and the press, with the learned professions, rankled in her mind until to get even with the arch enemy of the race became the prime object of existence. Men of sense have generally admired her earnest endeavor, and have shown a disposition to give her assistance, frequently saying it were better for humanity if women would generally spend more time upon the condition of public affairs and less upon dress, frivolity and household display. Chaucer, Ruskin, John Stuart Mill and May, with many other distinguished individuals of both sexes, have delivered the same opinions. The beauty of Mrs. Churchill's great work is that she never sought preferment for herself. Self-aggrandizement never formed any part of her policy. To do the work for which so few women are fitted by nature or experience was the height of her ambition. Her support financially must come from her endeavors, whatever they might be. Susan B. Anthony was liberally endowed for the work she did in behalf of her sex. Lucy Stone also received half the sum, sixty thousand dollars. Those women did noble work in the East, but did not accomplish the political emancipation of a single State.

Mrs. Churchill has performed a wonderful work under most difficult circumstances. It is not at all likely that another woman on the continent could under the same conditions accomplish as much. The simple, earnest plaint of the colored people carried an echo of woman's condition more or less pathetic. Those people say why do the ex-slave holders hate us? Did we not help to make their wealth? Did we not as servants give them a chance to educate their children and bestow upon them the best of opportunities? Why should they now hate us that we are trying to do something for ourselves? If we are ignorant and coarse, what have those people who make fun of us done to make us otherwise?

There is a note in this simple statement that strikes to the quick when woman is belittled by the press published in the interests of men exclusively. She has been man's slave. He has been educated at her expense. If he bought the ice cream, she was expected to pay for all his luxuries in reduced wages. She has done the drudgery and borne the insults of those who wronged her, assuming to be her protector. As woman becomes educated and influential this state of things to some extent disappears. The

81

foregoing causes was the incentive for establishing the little monthly paper called "The Antelope." Mrs. Churchill is a dear lover of animals, and knowing an order called after the Elk, not a delicately handsome beasty, thought Antelope rather better than Ursula, Bovine, Equine, Leoline, Feline, Canine or Porcine, she concluded Antelope would do. The paper was a monthly and very well edited. The facilities for getting out a paper in Denver thirty years ago were very poor, as the publishers had only the material for getting out their own productions. At length a firm of lithographers consented to get out the first edition. It was produced June, 1879. Mrs. Churchill called for the edition next day. A conceited little printer was to be at the office Sunday morning to deliver the edition to Mrs. Churchill herself, as it must be sold immediately. The printer took especial pains to let her know that he was a married man, so that there should be no serious misunderstanding. Mrs. Churchill was then in her forty-seventh year, and fool proof as well as man proof. She, however, thought the frankness of this stupid piece of humanity was a great novelty to say the least, as most Western men were always bachelors whenever a new woman appeared upon the scene. The edition of a thousand copies was all sold by twelve o'clock, at ten cents a copy, and the demand remained brisk after the last copy was sold. The type not being distributed, another edition was struck off, but not so hastily disposed of, as the first had been read at the rate of about ten persons to the copy. The lithographers can vouch for Mrs. Churchill's promptness in meeting all financial obligations as well as getting out her paper on time.

The little paper soon had a very fair subscription list, and some advertising. The expense of the paper was very high; the cost of living and rents was much in advance of what they were in more Eastern cities. In 1879 Denver had a population of about thirty thousand. Most of the population had not come to stay, so longed to get back to what they called God's country. This may have been a peculiar phase of pious slang, but people all through the ages have been taught that their own God was a very partial individual, bestowing blessings for the believers' special benefit. The common ear was, and always has been, deaf and blind to the smacking of commercialism in his Gods requiring belief. Faith is a part of

83

nature's requirement in the success of anything undertaken in life, whether good, bad or indifferent. People had no faith in the future of the city of the plains. It was supposed to be just a good atmosphere for weak lungs, and in some cases a good place to come in order to escape the mother-in-law, or any phantom from which the wicked flee. The population was very transient, and withal very democratic, in the dictionary sense of the term. "The New Rich of the West" found that they really needed a residence city in a climate and among people where they had labored the early part of their lives to acquire their fortunes. They wanted the social freedom to wear a cowboy's hat without giving mortal offense, and the Eastern nabob occasionally wanted to go a-fishing accompanied by his housemaid, and there was no reason that he should fear being mobbed in the quiet city of the plains. And Colorado is certainly the place to fish and hunt and have a good time for an outing, as there is so much sunshine and clear weather—nothing to interfere. In the early days of Denver's history the people were very sociable. Mrs. Churchill says many times she was obliged to leave the city for outside towns in order to raise money to pay her bills, be-

changed to a weekly it was thought best to change the name. "Queen Bee" became the popular name for Mrs. Churchill, many persons knowing her only as by the name of her paper, not knowing her real name. The greatest grievance the editor has to complain of is the habit of the mass of the people to confuse her publication with the Omaha paper called "The Omaha Bee." The Omaha paper is one of Nebraska's leading dailies, a Democratic paper opposed to every sentiment promulgated by the Denver "Queen Bee," or rather the Colorado paper of that name. The owner of this paper seems to have been born with the ability to transact business with men, and with a class of men worth calling upon. Women were not, generally speaking, so easily reached, and were not as liable to be provided with ready cash, and many had prejudices which were not worth the time to combat. It would seem that men in Denver in ye old time were afflicted with woman on the brain. Men have always been afflicted this way more or less, according to the scarcity of woman. It is strong evidence that she is of much more importance in man's economy than most men are willing to admit. In communities where women are in the ascendency men are fondled and favored in every

objection he had to a certain female relative was that she never "gave cause for fault finding." There is a world of human nature expressed in that simple sounding sentence. Really, too much perfection of character has a reflex action on the fellow who thinks he cannot get anything out of life worth while without playing some forbidden game. Mrs. Churchill's employes made themselves useful in caring for the wounded Chinamen, one of whom died upon the floor where her office was located. Mrs. Churchill was obliged to keep her office and home together, partly from the necessity of being away in the interests of her publication, and because the business was not sufficiently remunerative to keep up another establishment. The position was an easy one for the printer; he could take his own time and be really his own boss. There were always enough meddlesome people to make disparaging remarks about being employed and bossed by a woman.

Mrs. Churchill says if "help" need bossing they are not worth having around. She would never keep people for work who had to be called in the morning. If one cannot take sufficient interest in what one is paid to do, to get up in the morning, they had better be sent home to mother, who has

so sadly neglected their education. A high-priced
man was never employed, as there was not work
enough to keep one busy, as there was no job
work. At first a young printer was secured who
with another aspirant had been trying to make a
living by printing cards and doing odd jobs. The
time came when they could not pay their rent
and had nothing to eat. One of the young men
appealed to his home folks and secured money
enough to take him to his friends; the other had
no such recourse, so applied to a kind-hearted
old gentleman whose popular title was "Colonel
Sellers," one of the kind who substituted hope for
every real want that came to hand. The job was
secured for the young fellow, who proved to be
excellent help. The young man was a Hebrew
and been well brought up. He had left home determined to make his own way without calling
on his people. He proved to be respectful, trustworthy, polite and sober, very important qualities in an employe. When he came to the office
he was without means, or clothing suitable for
cold weather. As this became known, efforts
were made to fit out the printer with little regard
to waiting for wages to accrue. In the early days
of mining camps there is always reckless prodi-

gality as to material things. Denver was no exception to this rule. Mrs. Churchill noticed when E's washing was sent in that there were no drawers. In going out to business she saw something floating from a boarding house window, which she turned over with her umbrella stick and found to be a new pair of drawers, which had been discarded because too small for the original owner. These were taken to the needy and received with a thankful heart. Everybody who knows anything about a mining camp or the new distributing centers thereof knows how men make things fly when away from their natural guardians, wife, mother, sisters, cousins and aunts.

Good clothing could be picked up in sufficient quantity to have clothed a small army if there were no demand for uniforms. Unless the country is in the toils of a panic, Denver is always crowded. One night Mrs. Churchill returned from a month's trip outside in the interests of her publication, and made her presence known at the fastened door. The printer appeared carrying a lighted lamp, apparently greatly embarrassed; with apologies in bashful confusion, the young man stammered: "These boys had no

place to sleep, so I let them lie down here, not
expecting you home." The editor took in the situation good-naturedly, saying, "Do not distrub
yourself; as the boys are here, let them rest," at
the same time stepping over the prostrate forms
of from four to six youngsters, each of whom was
trying to get a foothold in the West. Mrs.
Churchill reached her own apartment, and the
incident was soon forgotten in a sound sleep.
When morning came the coast was cleared, not a
boy in sight; "they had folded their tents, like
the Arab, and silently stole away." The question
was asked, where will they get breakfast? They
will scatter to different boarding houses and
make their wants known. No woman ever forgets that she is the mother of the race. The substantial, sensible, practicable women should be
asked into every important council held by man
in the interests of the common good.

Boys need not go hungry in the West who can
wash dishes. Good, reliable help is always in
demand. Brisben Walker, a brainy little man
with a big head, was publishing a paper called
the "Inter Ocean" on the same floor of the building
where Mrs. Churchill's paper was gotten out. Mr.
Walker reminded Mrs. Churchill of Henry George,

CHAPTER IX.

REMINISCENCES.

One learns by hard experience that a new, sparsely inhabited country is a poor place to establish a paper, unless it should be a daily with stock company. Those who had leisure for reading bought their home papers from the East. A great, stalwart fellow stood upon the corner of Sixteenth and Lawrence calling out the names of the papers in a stentorian voice, "New York, Chicago, St. Louis and Cincinnati papers." In time the stalwart form and stentorian voice disappeared from the street. It was reported that he had bought a farm. Mr. Walker also disappeared from the block; it was reported that he had bought lands and had introduced alfalfa into the state of Colorado. The real early pioneer seems to be sadly lacking in the desirable quality known as faith. He needs some one to go ahead and prove by practical demonstration that things can be made to grow in one country as well as another. The early Californians did not believe that wheat could be grown in that country. The State is now one of the leading wheat growers of the United States. It had to be demonstrated by some one with faith and sufficient interest to make a success of the experiment.

THE GIFTED WIDOW.

Mrs. Churchill had her office and home rooms from a young widow who sublet the apartments from an old ignoramus who owned the building. The widow came to Mrs. Churchill's apartment with the complaint that the villainous old landlord was pursuing her with much persecution. The widow was frightened and in such a frame of mind that her complexion had a green appearance. The woman was a fine looking brunette. Mrs. Churchill is a person not looking for trouble, but when occasion requires it she can come to the rescue, take up the cross and bear off the victor's crown to the glory of the individual needing assistance. Mrs. Churchill said, "When he abuses you again call me; I will come to the rescue."

She came again with the same changed complexion and frightened look upon her face. Mrs. Churchill arose in anticipation and went to the door, where she met the heavy villain of this per-

ural talents for doctoring and nursing. Mrs. Churchill inspired her with the belief that she could educate herself by opportunity and application—prepare herself for a position worthy of her gifts. The courage prevailed, although there was a child five years old to be provided for. There was a boys' boarding school kept in Denver at that time; Mrs. Churchill, in behalf of the widow, called upon the proprietor and made arrangements for the widow to bring her child and assist about the boarding house and take private lessons of their best teachers, some of whom were women. In a few weeks the proprietor told Mrs. Churchill that this woman was one of the most promising young persons he had ever met; her native abilities seemed prepared soil for education which had been withheld until judgment was mature enough to readily grasp every opportunity. Some kind people offered to take the child to their home and care for him that she might be relieved of this much, that would give her more time to study. The child, young as he was, had the reputation of being remarkable for lovely traits of character, and the people seemed to think he was more of a comfort in the household than a trouble. "I told you so," said Mrs. Churchill, "soon as one shows a disposition to help develop character, along the lines sensible people know to be what you are naturally fitted for, help will come from very unexpected quarters. In due time other opportunities presented themselves. Before her acquaintances could realize it she had taken a course of medical lectures in Denver. Boston friends hearing of her struggles, and of her success, wrote for her to come to the aristocratic old metropolis and she should have help to finish her course. One day a leading judge of Denver hailed Mrs. Churchill to give a piece of information that he knew would please her greatly. A wealthy old couple were going to travel on a long journey. They wanted to take with them a doctor and nurse in one person. The widow was recommended. A recommendation from Denver was called for. The judge was the man for this occasion, as the widow had taken care of a member of his family when in need of the best to be had. The judge spared no pains in his letter of recommendation. Here again was this law of the secret of success demonstrated. The widow took the position at a good salary, and had the double blessing of having her young son with her.

a reasonable length of time for an answer and none forthcoming, he locked the office, leaving the key with a tenant in the block, with instruction that it was not to be given to other parties than the editor upon her return. One day the kindly old gentleman who found this job for the boy came to see how he was getting along. Himself a curbstone broker, knew how life went when doing business without capital. He, Colonel Sellers, found the door locked and a great accumulation of mail. Upon inquiring of some of the tenants, he found out the true state of things, and surmised that Mrs. Churchill had not received the letter, or she would have been home to get out the paper on time, as she was one of the painfully punctual kind of people. The Colonel obtained the address as near as possible, took chances and wrote. This letter was received, and Mrs. Churchill came as soon as the train could bring her. Floating help was obtained and the paper appeared on time as usual. *2O 3089*

About this time there appeared a woman upon the scene who was a member of the Editors' Press Association. She invited Mrs. Churchill to join; the response was, "No objection." Now this was the country editors' opportunity to humiliate the

woman who could come to their respective towns
and get a list of subscribers for her own paper
and sell a good package of papers besides. Consequently there was an understanding that the
applicant be blackballed. This was done to a
man, proving previous arrangement. Mr. Willie
Pabor was president of the Association. He
arose and asked the editors what objection they
had to Mrs. Churchill, saying: "She has accomplished in journalism what no man in this State
could do as an individual. Is the objection because she is a woman?" One of those editorial
lights arose with this brief answer: "No, it is
because she is not a woman." This was what in
elegant slang might be called "a dead give away."
Mr. Pabor called for another ballot, which was
cast, after the thing was understood, and there
was not a dissenting vote. Mrs. Churchill had
been informed of the first result, and remarked
that it was about what might be expected from
a class of men born of woman steadily taught
from generation to generation that mothers were
an inferior kind of animal, created on purpose
to perpetuate an inferior class of men, that there
should be no scarcity of day laborers. Mr. Pabor,
the poet laureate of Colorado, for years after

sent the literature of the Association, but Mrs. Churchill declined to have anything to do with a class of men so much below par with the women of the country. Mrs. Churchill is frequently solicited for some organization. She steadfastly refuses to join, although an editor who blackballed her declared it to be done "just for a joke." It is a wonder they had not said it occurred because they had been drinking. For a strong hold this is considered weak man's best refuge in time of trouble.

A TERMAGANT.

A drunken typographer had been dismissed. A middle aged woman called at the office asking for the place. This woman was about forty years of age, black eyes and black hair, a south of Ireland type, and rather comely. She proved a good printer, and efficient, but what a virago! Although she had expressed herself greatly pleased at getting the place, there was constant grumbling and fault finding. Mrs. Churchill concluded that she had been accustomed to a diet of sticks, stones, tin cans, or any other old thing in sight. The assistant was a Kansas girl, lovely in disposition as the other was terrible. This young lady had been employed to help about the mailing, to look after advertising and local collecting. She had taken up a claim in Kansas, and with commendable courage and energy had come to Colorado for higher wages than she could get at home. When Miss L. would talk as if she were an ignorant mountaineer showing off by bossing little niggers, Mrs. Churchill, finding a chance, assured the Sunflower girl by what consolation she could plausibly offer, saying Miss L. needed fresh air; that the confinement of the office made drunkards of men and viragoes of women; that if Miss L. had her fair share of the breath of life she would likely be a different person. She was in the habit of going to confession, so one day, in a softened mood, she related how her poor mother was a washerwoman, living in a shanty upon the hillside, and how she (Miss L.) in childhood amused herself throwing missiles at the neighboring washwomen's children. The Sunflower girl (aside) says: "Poor Miss L. No doubt she needs fresh air; she also needed early training as well." These two sufferers then concluded that one generation of fresh air and civilized training would hardly have worked an entire reformation. Then Mrs. Churchill, with a memory fifty years ripe, related to the Sunflower girl stories from real life about those termagants, and how they used to flourish before woman was permitted much education. Since woman has learned to read, this phase of human terror has almost entirely disappeared from the earth as we see it.

It is likely reading biography of the life and sufferings of the subject has had much to do towards changing the ideas of woman on the cure for the termagant habit. If men had memories long enough to remember these results they would ever be thankful that women learned to read, and thereby found some who had the fortitude to suffer martyrdom in silence until something could be done to change the condition.

Why a maiden lady should be such a scold was a great mystery to the editor and the Sunflower girl. Whom had she a right to punish, as she did not own an enemy to the race of her own? She just blazed away at any one in sight, without rhyme or reason. When in her lucid intervals, her sarcasm and viciousness were forgotten. If the Sunflower girl had been sufficiently experienced in printing, the South of Ireland would have been discharged, but experienced women printers were very scarce. Miss L. was perfectly aware of her opportunity and made the most of it. There was a serious matter to take into consideration in publishing a paper without some person sufficiently interested to see that the copy was properly overlooked and the correct thing for publication in that particular journal. Mrs. Churchill's editorials were sometimes garbled to suit the printers' ideas and to change the sentiment entirely. Unauthorized things were run in the columns. Those paid to look after these affairs were often found not trustworthy when the editor's back was turned.

Mrs. Churchill had to reach the principal towns in about five of these western States in order to keep the expenses paid by subscription. The real reason women have few papers is because of the reluctance of the business portion of the community to give a woman the advertising at a fair price and pay cash. Men in the same business seem to feel themselves greatly wronged if a woman has any source of income that relieves her from constant toil and drudgery. Women with incomes from money at interest are frequently spoken of as criminals, with no other reason than an outburst of jealousy of the party who, from the sex standpoint, own the earth.

A weekly paper never stands the chance in a large city that it does in a place not of sufficient importance to sustain a daily. Mrs. Churchill found it hard to collect at certain seasons of the year in a city of so many dailies. The extremely dull season occurs immediately after the holidays. Mrs. Churchill found small places less affected, as far as the newspaper work was concerned, than larger places, so left her business in the city and reached smaller towns where there was less ground to get over and where things could be accomplished more expeditiously. Mrs. Churchill was owing the girl printer one week's wages, $12.00, and explained that it would take a few days to raise this, as she wished to take in Montana, and the distance was considerable, would take a little more time than she cared to spend on the road, but Montana was a good point for her business and she knew it. This State favored woman suffrage, and has since bestowed the ballot upon its women, simply as the natural right of any person submitting to the law and paying taxes. Mrs. Churchill explained to the printer that it would be necessary for her to get out in order to keep the bills paid. Miss L. expressed no objection to taking charge during

yond a doubt that she had allies and had been supplied with means to get away, as the money sent by Mrs. Churchill had not been paid to her, as she refused any consolation short of breaking up Mrs. Churchill's business; the money sent to Dr. B., that she might be paid, was used to defray the expense of the trouble she had made. In the early stage of this persecution Dr. B. had written Mrs. Churchill that she need not return to protect her rights, but to keep on with her trip until ready to conquer some other world; that a printer was installed who was able to get out the edition and see it mailed properly. A few days previous the editor had written to the office to have the paper miss one week, and after this order had been cancelled, the printer set up the cancelled letter and had it printed. A printer receives something of a soldier's discipline in regard to obeying orders: "Follow copy if it takes you out of the window—even if the window is up more than one story." A printer is not of more importance than the soldier who made up the Light Brigade. California proved a hard place for a woman printer to find employment, and Miss L. wandered about looking for work until completely worn out, then she was taken sick, and for want of funds sent to the county hospital. In time she recovered and was returning to New York when she stopped off in Denver. She came to see the landlady of whom Mrs. Churchill rented, and was told that the editor finding so much persecution in the heart of the city had bought property out near the City Park, built a house and was making her home on her own property when at home; that she was yet obliged to be on the road most of her time in the interest of her publication, that in all probability she was now out on one of her business trips and could not be found if called upon. The landlord of the tenement had gone to the better world while this termagant was in California. After abusing the loveliest old lady one could imagine she finished her tirade by saying, "That it was a judgment upon her that she had lost her husband in the time she had been absent." "But he was an old man, Miss L., and we think nothing unnatural about the old dying," continued she; "we may hear of your death some time, and no one will think it a judgment upon the rest of us who are still alive." The vixen positively smiled as she contemplated the possibility of any one being punished at her taking off. Not many weeks

after Mrs. Churchill saw in a New York paper
an account of a woman by the same name, with
the Miss attached, who had walked out of an
open window of a building with many stories
and was picked up from the pavement. She had
bought some lots in Denver and made several
payments; all this she lost by her remarkable
deportment. This woman needed more fresh air.

A NEW PRINTER.

The paper did not miss an issue, notwithstanding an editorial proclaimed that it would. After
this phase of persecution Mrs. Churchill concluded it would be wise to have her office away
from the business part of the city where it would
be more difficult for the enemy to operate. Consequently bought a pair of lots on Race Street
near Eighteenth, three blocks from the City Park.
Five hundred was the price paid for the lots.
The profits were so small on the little monthly
paper that it took two years and a half of steady
hard work to get the property paid for. Mrs.
Churchill's books were more profitable, but Denver was found to be a very poor place at that
time to get out books, and she found that she
could not well operate the paper and handle the

books to advantage, so the books were slighted. The realty was satisfactory and it did not matter at what point of the compass the paper was gotten out, the expense of express work would be no higher than in the heart of the city—one of the heaviest items of expense in conducting the paper. Although Mrs. Churchill was six months behind time in the payment of that property, the man of whom she bought saw that she was doing all that could be done with her opportunity, so accepted her explanations and found no fault. There are a few men on earth who can treat a woman right if there chance to be no woman to influence them otherwise. Men are sometimes susceptible to influence the same as women are. Years after Mrs. Churchill met this real estate man, and as he now was known as a hopeless "Old Bachelor," Mrs. Churchill without his permission quoted the man who when he saw what a strife the rats and mice were making with his cheese, went to London to get himself a wife and tried to bring her home in a wheelbarrow, which did not prove a successful way of managing the bride. Mrs. Churchill probably got off this nursery rhyme in pure vanity and for amusement. The realty man took it in

111

high dudgeon and speaks to Mrs. Churchill no more. The next that will be heard of him is that he went East and died. Verily, the literal man is the funniest person on earth.

would consider this a great piece of arrogance, at the same time must admit that woman's influence in public matters has at times been very potent of results. The money making phase of her mission would gladly have been omitted entirely if it had been possible, but this could not be done. Women as a class have no money at their command with which to defend their interests. They by rights should have a paid lobby at Washington every session of Congress to look to the interests of their own sex. The paper has cost Mrs. Churchill a great deal of money and a vast outlay of most splendid energy. For this gift of exertion she gives heredity some credit, the climate of Colorado more. Altogether, she issued her paper eighteen years without missing an issue. But twice was it late in mailing during that time. Mrs. Churchill had experiences with printers who have a way of reducing copy producers whenever their vicious vanities are to be propitiated. Get the editor to buy some material that could not be used as represented, then tell it as a capital joke on superior intelligence. Low cunning is ever the resort of those with low ideals. Woman has so long been the slave of the race, when she does appear in the might of her strength to ask for better conditions she is looked upon as a monstrosity by the herd.

Colorado is by nature rich in a multitude of resources. There are fountains of wealth if one could but tap the source. Publishing papers in the interests of subject classes is not liable to bring much revenue. Help, like our neighbors, is not very stable in this Western country, constantly changing places and occupation. Once Mrs. Churchill was needing a printer, and in looking about, ran across the little fellow who stayed at the office to deliver the first edition and gravely informed Mrs. Churchill that he was "a married man." No doubt, as the years rolled by, he had got a different idea of the woman editor, whom he saw had other business than that of taking advantage of men. He evidently felt sold, and sore over it, as he promised to come and get the paper out, but never came near, nor did he offer apology for trying to make the paper late, although he well knew Mrs. Churchill's desire for promptness. In waiting for the fulfillment of the promise, it would take two printers to get the issue out on time. Mrs. Churchill just heaved a heavy sigh at being treated thus, went out like a little man, found some typesetters, and ran them in. The paper came out on time as usual. Those people having petty grudges for no real reason, were ever trying to head off this will to be prompt as all foolishness in a woman. With all these little meannesses, there were people, and many of them, who fully appreciated the efforts of the publisher, and in the usual way willing to give her a helping hand. Nearly always was she permitted to occupy a whole seat in the cars, as much of her editorial work was done when on the road. On the other hand, when the day coach was crowded and the smoker was not, Mrs. Churchill took up her quarters in the smoker, without fuss or feathers, until things could be arranged, which was done usually with promptness. The local agents of the railroad companies have been reckoned among her best friends. In one period of the paper's history a girl was employed who with varying conditions remained two years. She was perhaps twenty-five years of age—old enough to have some stability of character. As a general thing, women printers were hard to obtain, as there were many more men than women and the females were in great demand for wives and for service. The males were wont to garble copy when the editor was absent,

116

and if addicted to the drink habit they were more
liable to be petty thieves than women were. This
girl was also of Irish descent, born in South Carolina but brought up a Protestant. On the whole,
this girl was better help than the salaried class
of typos would average. There is a kind of coarse
familiarity, in some classes of people born and
brought up in the Southern States, which is very
repugnant to the Northern-bred person, especially one of English ancestry. These people have
a way of wishing themselves to be treated as
"sisters," perfectly innocent of the fact that well-
bred sisters are very careful about undue liberties
with sisters' packages, letters or effects generally.
All packages coming to the editor, whether she
were home or out on a trip, were opened by this
South Carolinian. People who read this will
wonder why Mrs. Churchill did not put a stop to
this thing; because there were many petty
grudges to contend with of a more formidable
character, it was not wise to multiply them. The
jealousies coming from a difference in possessions
is bad enough, but that coming from difference in
tastes, which are brought about by superior natural qualities, heredity, or better acquisitions of
knowledge, whether by opportunity or superior

acter was never again attempted. "South Carolina," true to national traits, hinted at persecution. Said Mrs. Churchill: "Did it ever occur
to you that this is a game that two can play at
as well as one? I have influence enough to drive
your brother from his clerical position, and force
enough to drive him entirely out of this city, if
I so desire." How innocently the printer girl remarked that she "would not like that." "It is
about what you will get if you undertake to im-
pose your brothers upon me socially." "They
are as good as anybody," was the very natural
rejoinder. Admitted, but I do not attempt to
place myself socially where I am not wanted.
The Arab follows his sweetheart to some remote
point, knocks her down and drags her to the tent
by the hair of her head, and in some instances
this constitutes marriage. Our method is a little
in advance of the Arabs. There are yet men to
be found who have not learned a better way. It
is a queer phase of human nature that if a person
cannot come to our terms she should at once be
exterminated, as we destroy troublesome vermin.
It is a queer world, any way; many of us never
get used to it. Lord Macaulay says there are
people born into the world whom the world is not

yet fit to receive. It is likely his lordship was thinking of Milton when he made this assertion. In this case there were petty spites and low cunning during the stay of the printer girl. One phase of this spite was to leave off the distinguished subscribers from the subscription list, or those known to be personal friends, as all paid in advance; this would have a tendency to damage the business as much or more than any other method. Another plan was to damage property not in immediate use, that there might be safety in delay.

Two headings had been gotten out for the paper, that when one was too much worn for use it could be laid aside for a fresh one. The stock not in immediate use was being overhauled one day, and the discovery made that a cold chisel had been freely used on this heading so that it was rendered entirely useless. A pair of book chaces were rendered useless if needed, without an outlay of money and time. The centre piece of iron was removed and thrown in obscurity beyond recovery. There were petty thefts, and damage to the amount of $40.00, which she had to pay at the final settlement. The printers used to say "The Queen Bee office" was a regular bonanza

because the editor was obliged to be absent so
much to raise money for expenses. There is one
more of the girl printer's tricks yet to be re-
corded. There was a load of brick for building
to be located. The girl printer was told at what
hour the brick would arrive. Mrs. Churchill was
unavoidably absent. The brick came as per agree-
ment. The girl went out to dinner and remained
an hour and a half, keeping a boy driver, a hot
day in August, waiting in the sun. When she
came the boy gave her some very strong talk,
saying that if she had remained five minutes
longer he would have unloaded the brick where
he was, and gone about his business. If the brick
had been unloaded at that point she would have
been obliged to pay for having them reloaded
and taken to destination. Mrs. Churchill con-
gratulates herself upon never having kept a teamster waiting five minutes over time in her life.
The punishment for a printer who could not get
along with conditions at the Queen Bee office was
to turn them over to a regular printing outfit,
whose boss had a very gentle monosyllable for a
cognomen. Never was there man so inappropri-
ately christened. The name was ———. He
seemed to be in a state of chronic indigestion at

to justify writing. There must be so much of carnage to interest the males of the race.

A boy from Kansas wrote that he was a printer and desired to come to Colorado in order to get better wages. Mrs. Churchill needing a printer about this time, wrote that if he neither smoked, drank nor ran around nights, he could come. He came. A cadaverous looking youth, with a uniform grey color predominating—hair, eyes, complexion and suit of clothing all seemed of one hue, as a boy of seventeen would be liable to look who had not had his growth and had been fed on low-wage diet. The boy of this age who has a mother to see that he is not overworked while growing, or underfed, can usually rejoice in a pretty presentable child, although he may not be what young girls call a "pretty fellow." Women generally should be taught that the rough life men must needs lead, in order to be healthy, useful and manly men, would preclude the possibility of a great degree of physical perfection, especially in color. It is not a bad reflection to know that in all probability the human animal has endowments enough without aspiring to be the beauty of all creation as well as the ruler.

The plain looking boy was installed with the ever-earnest and seldom fulfilled prayer that he prove at least a trifle more trustworthy than those who had gone before. Young people must have society, and without parental guidance they are liable to pick up any two-legged creature on the earth, and positively come under the influence of one who has not a single trait of excellence by which he could recommend himself, saying nothing about being well spoken of by others. These social tags usually are great critics in their own way. The printers had regular stages of education coming from outside influences. Mrs. Churchill became such an adept in this order of proceeding, from its frequency, that she had answers all "cut and dried" for the symptom first and last. The first symptom would show itself in the assertion that no woman could boss him, or her, as the sex might occur. The answer for this irresistible piece of logic would be: No help employed here who does not have the capacity to boss himself or herself, as the editor is obliged to be so frequently absent as to make it impossible for her to become proficient as a boss. Mrs. Churchill had no time to waste upon the neighborhood, so was never popular. Knowing, as she did, how the "Pin Heads" of the world amuse themselves, she had no desire for popularity. Of course, such women are looked upon as monstrosities by people not at all familiar with the type. The Grey-boy was found well enough in his knowledge of the business to get out the paper while the editor was absent. He was found to have some ability for composition, but was silent, secretive, covetous—just the qualities needed to make a shallow, petty thief. Mrs. Churchill says that it is her experience that the smaller calibers among men are so jealous of any success shown by women in business that they will do all in their power to head it off and steal from and rob her every time it is possible. This certainly makes an interesting world for her to combat with. There was once a state constitution formed by most competent parties for the State of Colorado. It contained a clause providing for magistrates who should be a salaried officer, whereby those wronged and not able to stand a law suit could have their grievances adjusted as well as possible without expense to themselves. There were women in the council called for framing this constitution. It was not adopted. Too much protection for the widow and the orphan. The Grey

Grey boy's father had visited him in Mrs. Churchill's absence. The secret drawer in the strong
box was too much for the boy, so he called his
paternal ancestor to his assistance. The boy had
such perfect confidence in his ability to deceive
the editor that he had on his watch chain an
emerald ring that she had in her stock, kept for
trading. He had done so much in this line, and
had nothing said about it, that he grew amazingly
bold. Mrs. Churchill called upon a big, stout
neighbor, by whom she had lived for several years
and knew him to be of the right material for such
an undertaking, and asked him to come and help
adjust the matter. He came, and Mrs. Churchill
confronted the boy with his stealing. One would
think a person with the courage to commit crime
enough to send him to the penitentiary would
have more "sand" than to break down and cry
like a great baby. This the Grey boy did. A
person who has not sufficient moral courage to
do what they will acknowledge to be the right
thing is every time a coward and a sneak. This
fellow was told that if he would confess all his
stealings that he would be permitted to take his
place in the postoffice, but that if any irregularity
was ever heard from that source, he would meet

127

with exposure of a most determined character. He then opened his trunk for examination. Books that had been sent to the office for review, sheet music, and many other articles for editorial notices were found. The ring he was wearing on his watch chain he stoutly denied having stolen; at last offered to surrender it. Mrs. Churchill told him of the record he had as a first class liar, and she further gave him to understand that she had never been deceived, for he had not the judgment to be consistent in his falsehoods. A falsifier has not well balanced common sense. The boy was charged fifty-five dollars for his stealings and permitted to go to his new position. If there chanced to be arrears in wages, the help had credit at the grocer's, which Mrs. Churchill provided when out on long trips. These things were well arranged, so that there should be no want or reason for dishonesty. The account at the grocer's was frequently a cause of great injustice to the proprietor of the paper. They Grey boy continued for several years in the postoffice, but at last was snapped up for falsifying, and left the country very unceremoniously. Mrs. Churchill wrote to the postmaster general and told him of the true character of the boy, and counseled

them never to give him any public office, as it is
doubtful, where father and son are of the same
stripe, if reformation is likely to take place.

There was a strain of malicious mischief in
the boy's proceeding as well as theft for gain.
A scrap book, which Mrs. Churchill had been
many years collecting, was stripped of all the
articles pertaining to her own career—many of
them files of her own short sketches, songs of
her own writing, and things that when destroyed
could not be replaced. When the boy was asked
what reason he had for malicious mischief, he
said, "No reason." He could not say why he did
it, unless it was to get even with the boss. "Did
not the boss," as you say, "provide you a good,
comfortable home and pay you better wages than
you ever had paid to you before?" Yes, these
points were all acceded. There is one printer,
an elderly man, who is old enough, and knows
by experience that the help in this office have
been more than well treated. He ever is ready
to put himself out to assist when there is need
for extra help in the office. The office was never
a straight-out Union office, but the help were always paid Union wages. This elderly man is not
under the influence of some outside "Pin Head."

or left at the city of Silverton until such time as it could be recovered. Mrs. Churchill had a trunk, in which she carried her papers for sale, her exchanges, a change of raiment, an extra wrap for occasions, a shawl and shawl strap. The trunk had seen its best days, and might as well be laid out in the San Juan country as to endure farther imposition, as it was now tied up with ropes and required a trunk surgeon, a professional, to get at the contents. The situation is not clearly comprehended until the place is reached, or the trunk would have been left at the boarding house, and the effects done up in the shawl and carried, as the emigrants used to do half a century ago. The short stage ride was delightful, but the end came, as was foretold. The passengers and mail were got out on the ground. Then there began a hurried scramble to see who would get there first. This was not the reason for the scramble. The real reason was that no one seemed to exactly be able to comprehend what came next. No one wished to be left in a place very long that might be peopled with mountain lions, bears, or even woodchucks. And, some way, every one seemed to think construction trains not as reliable as those running on schedule time. The man who had charge of the United States mail bags found more than he could handle without strings and straps, so that he might make a pack animal of himself for this rare occasion. He chanced to espy Mrs. Churchill's trunk and requested the ropes, as he knew no other way to overcome the difficulty of his task. Mrs. Churchill saw her way now to get those hard knots untied. While the mail man was doing up the great bags she was filling the shawl kept on purpose for such occasions. There was in the company an Englishman, about six feet high, who did not, as a general thing, trouble himself about what others were doing, either how, when or where. However, he espied Mrs. Churchill's luggage and remarked that "It will never do to leave the woman with all this luggage," and without waiting for a response took up a heavy satchel, and with long strides made off with it. "Dear me," said she, "here is one mountain overcome. I never could have reached the construction train with that heavy leather satchel and the shawl, which was swelled out of all possibility of the strap in which it was usually carried." A walk of a mile, during which the track layers would occa-

133

portunity, as she could accompany Mrs. Churchill, and the rest could be made possible. The
editor became interested in the girl, and asked
her if she was well enough educated to take
chances in the business world. She said she had
always lived in a new country, on a cattle ranch,
and her opportunities had been very poor. Said
Mrs. Churchill: "It will never do in this age of
the world. You must write a good hand, spell
well, read anything in the language of the country, and you must have a mathematical education; otherwise you go through life always feeling that you are handicapped, and that you have
been grievously wronged by some one, whose
duty it was to see you decently prepared to live
in the world, with the chance to make the best
of your abilities. What you want is a few terms
at a good public school." Mrs. Churchill was
soon to move into her own new house, and needed
capable help. A bargain was made, by which
the help was mutual. The girl was to manage
the cooking for her own board and room for the
winter. The fall term would begin in about the
right time to give a chance to move and get settled. There were one or two stops before reach-
ing Denver. The landladies, upon learning that

the young lady was going from house service to educate herself, would take no pay for her night's lodging and breakfast. This is given to show others how people will appreciate those trying to better their condition. No hotel bills for the struggling girl. To show how unsophisticated a girl could be, and still be one of more than average intelligence, this is related: She heard some one say that we would meet the other train at Chama. Although over public school age she knew nothing of the management of railroad trains, and was positively fretting because she could not understand how those cars were to pass upon one track. Mrs. Churchill explained the mystery of switching to the best of her knowledge, and showed the girl the futility of fretting about a thing she simply did not understand; that she must learn to have confidence in the general management of the world's affairs; that there were many things needing woman's help and counsel, even her command, but men had not been brought to see the advantage and were still blundering along at the same old rate, even in railroading, killing a fearful number of people every year, where many lives might be saved by calling women into their councils. Women have

136

learned that men are really capable of being made much more efficient for good works, and we can only work and pray and feed them to the best of our ability, to get better results than the world now dreams of. The girl proved a veritable treasure. When school term commenced there was some question about her age, as she was several years older than the law allows for public school favors. Deception was not to be resorted to. Mrs. Churchill would call upon the county superintendent and have the matter adjusted to suit the case. There were but two points to be discussed and Mrs. Churchill had won. A child is not to blame for being neglected. Some one is to blame, but not the child. Civilization is old enough to have had things better fixed for the entire world if there had been judicious management. Women would never have made a law prohibiting public education at any age when the victim might be prepared to avail himself or herself of its advantages. These two points settled the matter. Mrs. Churchill went to the bank with the girl, for the purpose of helping her about depositing her surplus earnings, sixty dollars, after reserving five for her books. How is this for a girl house-worker?

she was teaching in her home in San Juan county, near her mother, to whom she was very much devoted.

THE KINDERGARTEN CHILDREN.

Mrs. Churchill was one time coming down the street in Silverton, a broad, nice plank sidewalk. At a cross street she encountered about forty children, apparently of about the same age. They came down the hill like a flock of birds, but in remarkably good order. When they reached the corner they all stopped, as if under some command. Mrs. Churchill stopped, also, because the way was completely closed and the only thing to be done under the circumstances. The little folks just stood and gazed, as if looking at an unexpected curiosity. "Well, children," said the editor, "you are not used to white-haired old ladies, are you?" The gaze continuing, with no answer, she further said: "Do you think I am handsome?" One boy, a little larger than the others, said: "You are all right." Then, seeing the ridiculousness of the thing, the children were all in motion again, like a flock of birds, without friction, going together to the next crossing, then scattering, each for her own home. Mrs. Churchill says this was a pretty kind of a tableau, and, as there are many disagreeable things to record, it is only fair to the reader to have now and then something better than tragedy.

THE BROKEN GIRTH.

Once Mrs. Churchill was going from Telluride to some other point, the destination not remembered. The route led over the range, beyond the great snow basin, where a mail carrier was lost and his body not recovered for three years. An elderly man was employed to act as guide and furnish the means of transportation. Mrs. Churchill boarded in his family, always, when at Telluride. When the animals were being saddled something of an argument took place in the enclosure. This much could be heard at the back porch of the residence: "That girth is not fit to trust; it is old and tender," from a feminine voice. "I will use it," from a masculine voice. From the feminine voice: "Here, if you will insist on using that old girth, take this new one in your pocket, in case that gives way." "Very well," said he, and the new girth was deposited in a pocket and nothing more heard of the affair at that time. The means of transportation was a pair of mules, of excellent reputation for ami-

ableness and horse sense. The matron of the
house had gone out to see that everything was
done to make the journey a safe one for the lady,
who had made a home with them for years, when
out in the interest of her paper. Mrs. Churchill
had heard the confab about the girth, but paid
no more attention, as she had perfect confidence
in both parties, and knew the woman to be a person of excellent judgment. She knew, also, that
the man was much the oldest, and sometimes
querulous at supervision. The party had been
told about having "slickers," to wear about noon,
as there would be rain to encounter. Pandora
was passed. The beautiful cascade, the longest
in the state, that could be seen for miles from
the right direction, was left behind. Fearfully
narrow paths running around and along mountain sides were overcome, and the great snow
basin, before mentioned, where the body of the
lost mail carrier, with that of his horse and the
mail bags, were recovered, after the search of
three summers, conducted when the snow was
lowest and softest. For thousands of years these
great snow deposits have not been melted. These
snow basins form the heads of the rivers, that
unite and flow with such majesty through the

and some horse sense, it is admitted, knows more in a case of emergency than many a person. The creature had braced his fore feet and put his ears forward as soon as he knew something was wrong, and never budged an inch until the trouble was over. Then he whinnied to the other mule to let him know of his own narrow escape. The other mule had gone to grazing on a limited scale until he should be called for. Upon investigation, Mrs. Churchill found that she was not injured, only pretty badly scared. A three-cornered rent in her umbrella and a little mud were the worst of the damage. The new girth was produced from the left side coat pocket, and the journey resumed. Every year after this event, when Mrs. Churchill visited Telluride, inquiry was made about the faithful animals that took her over the range. If Mrs. Churchill had been a wealthy woman she would have given that mule, or the pair, a life annuity.

Before the days of many railroads in the southern part of the state any person doing a traveling business was obliged to take queer chances in transportation. Mrs. Churchill had come to the end of anything regular in getting about, but was told a team would be along such a time and that she could take passage with this, and by noon that teamster would branch out in another direction. But at this point a couple of young men would be found taking their dinner under a big tree. These young fellows were freighters and had one good saddle horse, which they took turns in riding, while the other one directed the pack animals. Mrs. Churchill was told that she could lay claim to the saddle horse "by right of discovery." She found everything as represented, only in one respect much better. The freighters were gentlemen and knew all about Mrs. Churchill's career, and received her as if expecting her. This might be so, and if brought about was done verbally by people carrying messages from one point to another when going on business. Messages were often of much importance, so that it was a part of this primitive life to lend a willing ear and execute the message faithfully. This time a lunch was taken along. The saddle horse was hers until four o'clock; two young gentlemen walked instead of one. At length the parting of the ways came for the freighting party and she must make a few miles more in order to reach her destination. What providence was to come to the rescue this time remains to be fulfilled. It came, however, in good time. Mrs. Churchill called upon the postmistress and was informed where she could get a horse, but a few rods away. The postmistress furnished her with a side saddle. Directions were given for the return of both horse and saddle. Mrs. Churchill took her mount, strung up her hand baggage to the saddle, and was off in as great a quandary as was the widow of the prophet, trying to save her sons from slavery, when she applied to Elijah for a method, and was told how to retail oil that she could not dispose of at wholesale.

The horse proves to be a sure-footed beast, young and able, so that the journey came to a close at dusk, and there at the big stable yard was a man waiting to take that horse back to the little berg where Mrs. Churchill obtained it. The saddle was not even removed. In these mining camps the people seem more like a congenial family than a conglomerate of different nationalities. The segregation and the isolation work wonders in the socialistic line. The same principle upon which the family is reared in domestic life: there must be honor and confidence in that honor— neither is often violated. Another time Mrs.

Churchill, because of diverging roads, was left at the roadside with her hand baggage, something as poor Hagar, only without Ishmael. She had been told that a drove of horses would pass that way at this very hour. They had been driven up the mountain loaded with tourists and were returning to their stable saddled and bridled. Mrs. Churchill did not wait more than ten minutes, when there came that drove of fine looking horses, in the care of an intelligent man, and there was but one side saddle in the lot. There were two other men, one of them a tourist. Mrs. Churchill hailed them when at some distance, as the horses make very good time when going down hill. The men and horses come to a stop; the affair is understood, as likely other women had availed themselves of this mode of transportation, and men, too, for that matter. The company were quickly mounted, Mrs. Churchill placed in the lead—a way those mountaineers have of showing deference for the wiser sex. The man in charge said, "Dear me! She can ride as well as write." The destination was reached in safety.

A reader might wonder why a newly settled country was chosen for a work of this character. Because all reforms take root in new countries sooner than in older communities, and in inaccessible places there is not the same means at hand for getting rid of money. There is more money in the community and less competition. Older communities are always filled with reading matter of long standing.

CHAPTER XII.

Ironton and Ouray.

One of the finest pieces of scenery (outside of
the Grand Canon of the Arkansas) in the state
of Colorado. The sublimity, grandeur and ter-
ribleness of the route is all the terror-seeking
tourist will ask, as a usual thing. Thirty years
ago the road was a mere trail. As it is a county
road the trail has been widening as county work
could be done, until it is now a good carriage
road, with a prospect of railroad in time. The
work is, of necessity, slow because of solid rock
on one hand, rising hundreds of feet perpendicu-
larly. There are sections of this highway where
every foot of this rock must be blasted in order
to make the huge notch required for a passage.
Below this there is a precipice of such frightful
depth as to take one's breath at a careless glance.
There runs a mountain rivulet at the bottom of
this declivity, and the distance is so great that
the stream is to the eye not much more than a
silver thread. If anything occurred to locomo-
tion upon the narrow road the victim must take

the journey down that precipice, without a twig
or growth of bunch grass to stay his deadly trip.
The eye takes in all these possibilities at a
glance, and the fear would be fully equal to meeting a grizzly bear without means of defense.

A PERILOUS TRIP.

The first time Mrs. Churchill went over this
route she firmly believed that it would be the last
time. But each succeeding year brought improvement, which was reported, and the trip would be
undertaken again rather than to go five hundred
miles around by rail, which would consume much
time. There were a loyal host of subscribers to
her publication at Ouray, a point of too much
importance, from a business point of view, to be
ignored for precipices or any other thing. The
first time the road was traversed by Mrs. Churchill was going from Ouray to Ironton. There were
a couple of livery men consulted, one whose
name was Nutter, and "Highwayman" will do
for the other. As the old files of the paper are
on file at the State House, Denver, the data is
not every accessible, or the name would not be
withheld. The bargain was made for Mrs.
Churchill to be carried as far as Rose's cabin

for the sum of ten dollars. This was the contract with liveryman Nutter and the money paid in advance. When the hour came for the trip another man appeared upon the scene, and the journey was taken on a donkey, the man walking. He was fully informed as to the contract, but made himself as disagreeable as possible about a small satchel, to be carried in his hand over the most dangerous part of the road. After the worst part of the trail was gone over he said he knew nothing of her contract with the other liveryman, and that he must have five dollars for his trouble, or we would turn back and consult Mr. Nutter, well knowing that the editor would not have traversed the route again for that sum. The fellow got the money, but something besides that he did not bargain for, for the next issue of the paper gave the particulars of this transaction in pseudo verse, or doggerel. Year after year Mrs. Churchill saw those fellows grow poorer in business until very ragged; then they disappeared altogether and went to some new field of action. A record is made of this case for its rarety among the mountaineers, as they were usually of·a different order.

IRONTON AND OURAY.

THE PROFESSIONAL MEN.

Once when this road had been enlarged to the dignity of a carriage thoroughfare Mrs. Churchill was going from Ouray to Ironton, and there were as passengers two professional gentlemen from Michigan, one an M. D., the other a dentist. Both suffered with fear. The best that either could do was to ride with one foot out of the vehicle, ready for a foothold, if nothing more, in case everything did not go off harmoniously. They were so located in the wagon that one had a foot towards the precipice, the other towards the impenetrable wall, as unscalable as the precipice was unavoidable. There was in either case no chance to be saved in case of accident. Those men could be heard, in a drowning sigh, to say: "Ever catch me going over this road again!"

THE SNOWSLIDE.

The snowslide visits this section frequently. In winter great caution is necessary to use the road at all. These slides take everything in their path, and go over this highway without sinking into the roadbed, making a beautiful snow roof, with open ends, so that for months teams go through as a tunnel is traversed. Mrs. Churchill has been twice through this snow tunnel in the month of August. The warm air of summer causes melting of the snow inside the tunnel, so that it forms in beautiful, regular geometrical figures, as regular as if the imprint were made by a skillful artist. Natural law is a great artist when dealing with snow.

"BILLY," THE SNOWSLIDE LAMB.

Once a miner was plodding his way homeward towards Ouray and found a tiny specimen of a mountain lamb. He placed it inside his coat and quickened his step to the town. A grocer gave him sixty dollars for the little creature. It was carefully reared and the pet of everybody, even the dogs. One time the editor was looking after the interest of her publication, and was talking to some one on the walk, opposite to where the mountain sheep was standing. Said she: "What horns Billy has developed in the last year! Is he not dangerous to be at large?" "Not at all," said the person; "he has never yet made the least trouble, but is as playful with dogs as with people." The sheep seemed to know that the parties were discussing him. He came across the street and laid his big horns against

Mrs. Churchill's skirt as gently as possible, as much as to say, "I am not a dangerous lamb." She rubbed his head and patted him a little until he thought they were friends, and walked off as if perfectly satisfied that he had made the correct impression. The next year when Mrs. Churchill went down she inquired for Billy, and was told that he eventually became cross and was considered dangerous, so his owner had him taken to a high precipice, in sight of Ouray, where a flock of mountain sheep had lived securely for years right in sight of the townspeople. The elevation is so great as to make the members of the flock look about the size of house cats. Billy had behaved very well for a snow-slide waif, brought up without parental influence.

CHIEF OURAY AND HIS WIFE, CHEPITA.

For several years after Mrs. Churchill's visits began at Ouray the Indian chief of that name was still living. His wife Chepita was well received at our national capital, whither her husband sometimes had occasion to go in the interests of his tribe. The Washington ladies used to dress her up in Indian costumes, but of rich material. Her appearance was so picturesque as to teach a

153

national lesson, that beauty or style need not be confined exclusively to any one portion of the race. Mrs. Churchill finds in her neglected manuscripts a little song written years ago, upon the second marriage of Chepita, and from its sentiment infers that it was not customary for a widow of that tribe to take to herself a second husband, but that it became imperative in order to protect herself from the intrusions of the ruling race.

MARRIAGE OF WIDOW OF CHIEF OURAY.

Chepita the wife of Ouray,
How could you so far go astray
As to marry another man, pray?

The Ute has a finer conception
Than the white man of human perfection,
And it is likely Chepita's deflection
Came about by the way of reflection
Upon the white man and his ways.

Chepita, beloved of her race,
The pet of the whites for her grace,
Has lost forever her place,
By a mixture of customs of race.

women of some tribes were better marksmen than the Indians were, and were superior at managing the canoe, but were never permitted to join the games where there were prizes offered for contestants. The explanation was that a class holding themselves to be superior did not want to come in competition with a class considered inferior, because if excelled the humiliation would be doubly embarrassing. Mrs. Churchill was fond of the great, silent forest and would have liked hunting, and probably found some excuse, as humane hunters often do, for killing the animals that had never given offense. Next to hunting came beech nutting in the fragrant woods. A poetical nature would hear music in the rustling leaves, the pigeon's lone cry, as most of them have gone south, and the blue jay's plaint, which is usually of a nature indicating loneliness. The maneuvers of the blithesome squirrel, the enjoyment of the roving pig, all contribute to make a paradise of earth for a few hours at least. Young life is so redolent with hope. The world with its terrible crosses is going to yield up such a fund of happiness, if we only have the patience to wait. Nature keeps us waiting, with an occasional glimpse of the rainbow, and fools us along where

ically treated with the old-fashioned salaratus and a little salt, and meat fryings for shortening. This compound was worked with flour in a small wooden bowl. When the consistency was right, rolled out and baked in the ashes. The women likely had no oven, not even the old-fashioned bake oven. Hot ashes were drawn out upon the hearth of an open fire-place, of the most primitive pattern. The hearth was of large grey stones. The cake was placed on the cold ashes drawn over the hot embers, then cold ashes put on top of the dough, and hot embers covered the whole. There was nothing to do but wait. Children in those days were taught to be seen and not heard. The whole party was a very silent one, likely from extreme fatigue on the part of the children. The woman had not uttered a sound since the party were seated. The eldest sister had some few remarks to offer on what had been seen in the dark, silent woodland. After some patient waiting (mostly because too fatigued to be restless) the cake was silently taken from the ashes and brushed off with a clean cloth, broken in pieces to suit the number to be served, butter from a scant quantity was put upon each piece, and the

were prepared up ahead and on hand. Ice was not in general use; the clean, spacious cellar answered to some extent the same purpose. The out-of-doors milk house, with running water in the bottom, was also an ideal place to keep food in warm weather. The meat roasts, the roast pigs, geese, ducks and wild game, cooked in that big brick oven leaves a savory memory at least. The custards and Indian puddings, with baked fruit and all vegetables that were "bakable." There was in this home a large oak chest with two spring locks. Just such a receptacle as caught the bride of Mistletoe fame that was missing for twenty years. This great chest was used as a store house for the maple sugar, and a good supply of honey was also in store. Mrs. Churchill's mother was Holland and German stock, transplanted to Pennsylvania soil, where housekeeping was brought to a great state of perfection a hundred years ago. Mrs. Churchill's parents were busy, earnest people. For many years the family about the board numbered nineteen people, including apprentices, children, grandchildren and invalids, being treated for almost any ailment to which flesh is heir. The father and mother were well calculated to keep a hotel or sanitarium; just what they were doing without being conscious of the fact. If teeth were to be extracted the mother could do a plain piece of dentistry as well as the doctor, who was ten miles away when at home.

CHAPTER XIV.

MAPLE SUGAR.

The season for tapping the trees was ever a season of joy. One learns the kind of weather required to make the sap have the best runs. It was the weather that produces acute catarrh, so that the running of sap came to have a double meaning to children. The sugar bush had charms because of the novelty, and because the whole world is new to children and most charming. When one gets a little experimental comparison the thing is seen in a different light. The baby's song reads, "Sleep, little bird, and dream not why."

It was learned later that father's sugar works were not equal in size to some of the neighbors', as they manufactured for sale; the other was only for family use. This was a great surprise to some of the house, who had an idea that the largest family in the neighborhood should certainly be equipped with the best facilities for the sugar business. An elderly woman who had been widowed about a year, was asked how she pros-

162

pered? She answered, "Very well, only we do not
have as much 'sweetening' as when father was
alive." Mrs. Churchill dreamed over this simple
human story, imagining how the poor old man
became stooped in his shoulders, carrying sap
with a neck yoke, and doing the work years after
he was really not physically able to do this class
of labor. Then missed more for his sugar pro-
ducing ability than for anything else. She finally
concluded that this miss was a better hit than
every one makes, as some are only missed for
utter worthlessness. The children were mostly
at school, and had little to do with the general
exercises of the process until sugaring-off day
came, which was usually in the afternoon, and
sometimes late in the evening, as this job could
not be deferred to a more convenient season. The
mother superintended these occasions, saying
that the men folks were liable to let the sugar
burn, and that would render the batch only fit
for vinegar. Once the family returned home at
dark, all having been out at the finishing process
and eating warm sugar until as hungry as young
wolves for a good supper. The hoods worn in the
bush had not much more than been laid aside
when supper was announced. What a surprise;

163

there had been no one left at home to attend to this matter. The meal was a boiled dinner, really, the best calculated to appease a sugar-surfeited appetite. This very welcome and much appreciated supper was for several days discussed by the elder children of the household, as if it had been a miracle. There was no one at home to attend to this matter, and it was months before it was disclosed that a party had been promised a big roll of sugar on a freshly cut hardwood chip for attending to that meal, and having it cooked by the time the family returned. The vegetables were prepared early, and a child was sent to tell when the sugaring-off business would be over. The party was a neighbor and had duties of her own, was the reason it seemed so mysterious. This effect was more accidental than anything else; the mother, enjoying the situation, did not explain until the roll of sugar on the chip was discussed by the recipient; then the matter was gradually unfolded. The big cakes of well grained maple sugar were placed edgewise in dishes that caught the molasses, as the drainage was called, to be served with hot griddle cakes. The great oak chest was the storehouse for sweets.

About this time a carding mill was established not far from Mrs. Churchill's home. The innovation was a great curiosity, because the women had hitherto carded their own rolls and spun them; now things were to be different. The spinning of both wool and flax Mrs. Churchill had seen done on a limited scale in her own family. There was homespun forthcoming and worn, but not to the extent of that of some communities. The author learned to knit socks and stockings, but the manufacturers were upon the country and there was not much home-made clothing after 1845. She remembers a blue and white linen dress, home made, in which she kneeled to say her morning prayers at the family altar. This goods when freshly ironed shone with a luster like silk, and was thought to be very pretty. In one of these freshly ironed linen dresses she made a visit to a much beloved niece. There had been building going on, and a pile of bricks was an irresistible inducement to teach the niece, of about the same age, to make chimneys that would draw, and brick ovens that would bake, though not as large as the grown folks had. The business was pushed with such energy that the time for dinner was not taken into consideration, and when the call came, the front of the little aunt's dress was about the color of the bricks, the material having been transported with a familiar hug against the newly ironed linen dress without regard to consequences. Children are often more earnest in the work called play than grown people are in real work, hence some insignificant thing is liable to be overlooked, for which grown folk would prepare. Dinner was announced. The situation was little short of terrible, as the freshly ironed linen was in such a deplorable condition as to be unfit to appear at any one's table. The niece was a child of resources. She brought a clean, bleached linen towel and a paper of pins. By pleating one end of the towel the right size a bib was tastefully improvised that concealed all the evidence of the wearer having been engaged as a common bricklayer. For this little feat in overcoming a serious difficulty the young folks received congratulations.

twelve years of age, and hearing a commotion in the lower rooms, arose from her bed, went down stairs, opened a crack in the door far enough to watch proceedings, and from this makes her report. The mother seemed to do a moment's earnest thinking, then said she: "There have been two pairs of turnkeys left here to be delivered to two doctors living in an adjoining township. If you are willing, I will pull the tooth and end your suffering." He sat down in front of an open fire-place, the light improved by a handful of lightwood. A darning needle was used to remove the gum, as there was not a suitable knife at hand. The instrument of torture was wound with a red silk handkerchief, for the better protection of the gums. The instrument was placed upon the top of the root and out came the offending tooth, striking the hearth. The man jumped to his feet and spit in the fire-place. And while examining the tooth that had given so much pain he exclaimed: "There is a hole large enough to drive in a span of Norman horses and turn around!" After putting a pinch of salt in the wound there was a bill passed into the hand of the operator; there were profuse thanks upon the young man's part that a woman could

be found with sense enough to be cruel in order
to be kind. Another pair of tooth keys were sent
for, these being kept for further service in the
immediate neighborhood. Mrs. Churchill has
those very instruments in her cabinet of curi-
osities. It is sixty-five years since the first tooth
was taken out with them.

Once Mrs. Churchill was at Pueblo in the
interests of her paper. The trunk containing
her material for business had not been sent to
her boarding place, the parties in charge making the very lame excuse that as it had been
snowing she would not be likely to need the
trunk or the contents. When people talk about
the business of other people they seldom know
a single point of the things they are merely
speculating upon. She rushed off to the depot,
but to find the man in charge of the baggage
gone to his home, as these were the days before Pueblo had a union depot. Mrs. Churchill
followed on to catch him there, but to be told
that he had returned to the office. While in the
house the snow drifted in such a way that she
could not open the gate. The location was rather
remote, and as the day was stormy, there were
few people out. The house stood on an elevation

several feet above the street; it was surrounded by a picket fence; the snow hid this fence from sight as well as the gate. She concluded that there was but one way out of the difficulty; that was to lie down and roll over the fence to the road. As she wore a heavy wool plush cloak, that distance of twenty or thirty feet could be overcome without serious injury to person or clothing. The feat was successfully accomplished, the trunk released from check, and in a short time accessible so that business could go forward as usual.

Mrs. Churchill was at Las Animas, Bent county, stopping at the Gardner House. In the night she was awakened by the smell of smoke; she arose and raised a curtain, to find a brisk blaze rising as fast as possible to the roof. She had in early life taken down the high tones of her voice, used so much by the U. S. A. women to the great disgust of cultivated foreigners. In this accomplishment she had made use of what she called an elocutionary whoop. This queer noise would arrest a band wagon, if the performers had never heard it before. One of those signals, followed by the cry of fire, brought the traveling men in their night clothes to the lower hall, where the landlord had by this time appeared, and with the available water at hand, mostly from pitchers, the flame was brought into subjection until entirely extinguished. A scoundrel had been hired to burn the house because of business jealousies. He was to receive thirty dollars for the job. When it was found to be a failure the party of the first part refused to pay the money, so the party of the second part sneaked about until he got a chance to steal the amount he was to have if he succeeded. This led to the arrest of the party of the second part, and a trial followed, and the reader will be obliged to get the outcome of that trial from Bent county records, as Mrs. Churchill thinks both parties escaped punishment, when in all reason both should have been sent to the penitentiary. The hotel was a handsome frame structure, built by a widow who had brought up three children by her own exertions and was a first class citizen. The landlord at the time of the fire was her second husband and a prominent citizen. At this house Mrs. Churchill was entertained, ever after that, free of expense. The property would not have been a loss to the family alone, but a loss to the county seat of Bent county.

CHAPTER XVI.

THE SILVER PANIC.

In the year 1893, when the State of Colorado was suffering from what is known as the silver panic and remembered with a shudder as a dreadful calamity, Mrs. Churchill discontinued the publication of her weekly paper. Nearly everything was discontinued in the State, unless it should be the movement of tramps. There was nothing to do, and nothing to do with. The silver mines, the principal industry of the State, were shut down. Mrs. Churchill had a few pet chickens and a cat, with which to break the monotony. Owning her home, she had no rent to pay, and the dullness of the time gave her leisure to thoroughly overhaul the office and the whole place. She found plenty of clothing put away in barrels; old umbrellas in the garret. Most of us know how well paid girls will dress and lay aside their things when no longer in shape to be worn, making no more use of them because they either have not the time or do not know how. The young are not yet educated in the matter of caring for wearing apparel, nor in the importance of this branch

172

of thrift. Mrs. Churchill always walks with an umbrella as a cane. While she is not really lame, she is not strong on her feet. She could never make a successful skater on either ice or rollers because of this infirmity, which was never known, even in her own family. This accounts for the collection of umbrellas. Mrs. Churchill found, as winter approached, she was in need of a good, warm hood, so cast about for material for a door-yard bonnet. There were half a dozen mailing tables covered with batting and oilcloth. Some of those could be dispensed with. The batting would do for hood making, although in the mass of material at hand there was some available wadding. Mrs. Churchill had in her early youth learned something of millinery and dressmaking, for her own personal appearance. After constructing her hood, which was wadded with the filling of a discarded mailing table and lined with a resurrected umbrella, there was an unexpected demand for hoods. Twenty of those winter conveniences were made and placed before the supply of material gave out. Where the cloth was a substantial black, if an umbrella cover, it was washed, starched and nicely ironed, making better goods for linings than we usually buy. There were old ribbons enough, cleaned and restored with diamond dyes, to make bows and strings for a regiment of hoods.

No one ever heard Mrs. Churchill complain of being lonesome. She says in a world where there is so much to be done the lonesome business is more or less a want of will or ability to adapt oneself to the needful conditions by which every human being is constantly surrounded. A downtown gentleman once asked Mrs. Churchill how she entertained herself through the long, dull winter. By reading good books, writing, practicing music, feeding chickens and talking to pets. The next morning in Mrs. Churchill's alley, one block south, was found a lady dog tied to a post, and in a cheese box near were six young puppies. The family were blooded stock, and Mrs. Churchill always associated this outfit as a supplement to the pet business; only the person delegated to locate the dogs missed the intended residence by about one block, but had the correct alley. The humane officer was called and the dogs all chloroformed. The person who owned the property nearest where the dogs were located felt greatly injured at this treatment, although some one tried to prevail upon him to think that it was more dogmatic than hostile. Life is filled with wonderful mysteries. We are only obliged to wait the judgment day, when the graphophone of the universe shall be set in motion and some of the Denver men will call for the rocks and mountains to fall upon them, rather than listen to their own preserved plottings.

And when they have been there ten thousand
    years,
  Bright shining as the sun,
There will be no less days
To stand the blaze
  Than when they first begun.

We are taught for a comfort in this life that in the future there will certainly be more equity in distributing justice; that fully one-half of the judges shall be of either sex, so that all law and custom shall not be made in the interests of part of the race and executed for one party's whims, to the detriment of the other party's rights. In the future life no such condition shall prevail. Blessed hope! Let us believe and be resigned! It seems to be all that can be done with this world of mud and smoke upon such a gross plane—that our only hope for better conditions is located in the future.

CHAPTER XVII.

NEW MEXICO.

Mrs. Churchill was once at Georgetown, N. M., twenty-five miles from Silver City. The drive to Georgetown terminated in the afternoon. The people in this mining camp were preparing to amuse themselves with a dancing party. Mrs. Churchill never attends these places. If she had a taste for this class of amusement she would not be able to participate, because not able from a physical standpoint to endure as much work as was really essential to the welfare of her business, aside from dissipations. After supper Mrs. Churchill retires for the night, very thankful that the hall where the party was to be held was no nearer, as a tired traveler thinks more of rest than the whine of a poorly played violin. The great mass of people are not capable of comprehending anything much beyond their own environment, hence one of different tastes from themselves is considered a monstrosity, only needing discipline to be brought to think as others do, and act as others do. The old beer drinkers and whiskey tipplers of almost any country have been known to speak of a teetotaler as a man deserving to be obliterated or banished from the common

benefits of segregated society. But above all
things, a woman must not be tolerated in with-
holding herself from popular doings. On this
occasion Mrs. Churchill was not long in finding
out that she had incurred the displeasure of the
multitude by withdrawing to her own apartment
instead of going to the entertainment, although
she had not been served with an invitation. She
was treated as men sometimes treat women for
not proposing when lacking the courage to do so
themselves—take it out in petty revenges. As
the night wore on, it became evident that a boy
had been stationed upon the uncarpeted steps to
strike them with a whip from the limb of a tree,
so as to prevent any one from sleeping. When
these things occurred, which was not infrequently
in this land of the people, by the people and for
the people, meaning the males of the race exclusively. It was found best to keep perfectly
quiet, and get as much rest as was possible under
the circumstances, as business is business, which
takes strength to perform. Finally one of the
crowd had become well fired up with explosives
and came in front of Mrs. Churchill's room door
and delivered himself of some trite U. S. A. isms.
The victim of this tragedy had noticed a five-

177

quart lard pail standing on the stove, where some one had left it after bathing. The door was hastily unlocked and the contents, very convenient to the door, deliberately poured over the offensive party. Mrs. Churchill knew by his drawl that he was not likely to make any very active demonstration, so stepped back in her room, locked the door and listened for developments. The hall was without carpet, and the dripping water could be heard in the stillness nearly all over the house. The inquisitor with the whip was convulsed with laughter, and every effort on the part of the other silent spectators was in vain; the boy lay down on the hall floor as if in a fit, and laughed until his merriment became so contagious that Mrs. Churchill herself laid upon her bed and laughed heartily. Anything will go if a joke upon the other fellow. The situation became doubly ridiculous because the fellow was hardly able to get away without assistance. Mrs. Churchill obtained about four hours of sleep, in spite of the disagreeable occurrence. If women could have a hand in executing the laws for their own, these shameful performances would become of rarer occurrence. Men have given women the reputation of not being able to keep secrets.

The editor has taken them at their word and has told the whole unjust story every time it became justifiable. At the breakfast table Mrs. Churchill told the landlady that it was her duty to have stayed home, or delegated some competent person to remain in the house to see that her guest was not molested. The woman made some apology in self-defense, and the editor went forth in quest of subscribers for her publication, also to sell her book. The incident was the talk of the town. Mrs. Churchill was informed by respectable parties that there were plottings for the night to come, and that it would be wise for her to get through in time to leave, as the element was such that she could not very well be protected. The stage was tri-weekly and would not leave for Silverton until next day in the morning. Mrs. Churchill looked about for teams that might be going to the other town, but found none. In making up her mind that she might have some walking to do in this affair, she paid her bill and ate no dinner, as this is the best condition for a warrior when exhausted and with another battle in prospect. She took her hand baggage, about forty pounds, and began a journey which might have ended in death, or what is worse. There is

Some philosopher has said that out of our miseries springs our best happiness. In this case natural law was verified; the reaction had set in, and she remembered another woman who, eighteen hundred years ago, had been obliged to flee from tyranny, and, the story says, on the back of a donkey. Mrs. Churchill's chief anxiety now came from fear that the poor little beast they were riding would be broken in two, as the weight it was carrying was not less than three hundred pounds. She raised a protest against the spurs from the first, that the animal should not be abused from the results of her individual misfortune. The Santa Rito mine was reached. In a second the Mexican had alighted; helped his charge to the ground, also. Mrs. Churchill says she never beheld a quicker action than that of unstringing her baggage. By this time the postmaster was at the door. A confabulation took place. The postmaster spoke Spanish with ease, and requested the Mexican to not hasten away, as his services might be further needed. He then informed Mrs. Churchill that she was not safe in that place, as the distance was but a short one for spite to overcome; that at such a residence she would be able to hire a buggy and be taken in to Silverton. With this understanding the Mexican was requested to continue with her until some other conveyance was obtained. The Mexican strung up the baggage as quickly as it had been undone. The postmaster had heard the story from the out-going stage in the early morning. If Mrs. Churchill had heard of the threat in the morning she would have left that morning. By remaining but half a day gave her time to run up a subscription list that would have done credit to any paper. All was paid in advance, and mostly in silver, which added to her burden when climbing the long hill. She had the names of every one of those low villains. One man said he would "be glad to always buy her books and take her paper, but that she went through the country so boisterously." Mrs. Churchill is anything but boisterous, either in voice or manner. The fellow did not know what else to say. She was again in the Mexican saddle, going to look for a conveyance to take her to Silver City. The couple had gone but a short distance when they met a large load of wood, piled so high they are never expected to turn out. Coming from Georgetown was a livery team, with two seats and two occupants. Both the liv-

183

ery team and the Mexican had driven the fore feet
of the animals into a stone pile made by road
improvements. It took a minute for the wood
load to pass. In the meantime Mrs. Churchill
asked if they were going to Silverton. The answer was affirmative. "Would you take a passenger?" was the next question. "Certainly,"
said the gentleman, who was his own driver.
The Mexican could not have acted quicker if he
had been master of English. He saw through it
instantly, alighted and took the baggage off the
donkey, and by the time Mrs. Churchill was in
the vehicle the stuff was also in, ready for movement. She reached for her purse and handed
him a ten in gold. He only shook his head and
smiled. Then a five in paper. He would not
touch either. By this time the livery team began to move. She took his outstretched hand,
and sent every sentence of Spanish at him she
had ever learned, however inappropriate some of
the lingo might have been. The Mexican laughed
and passed out of sight, waving his hand and
bowing in response to her demonstrations. The
couple in the conveyance were too much interested in one another to give Mrs. Churchill any
attention, a condition for which she was very

thankful, as there was need of quiet and mental repose. At five o'clock the destination was reached. She was driven to the boarding house where she had made her home while "doing" Silverton. That evening she had the adventure written up and in the mail for her weekly paper, with the names in full of every one connected with the *tragedy*. Mrs. Churchill was once at Georgetown since that occurrence. Not one of the same inhabitants were to be found. There was some kind of a gathering, and the women requested her to speak for them, which she did to the satisfaction of those in charge. Mrs. Churchill was in that section of country when Mr. and Mrs. McComas were killed by the Apaches. She passed over the same road the day before, and dined at the same wayside inn, where the little girls were left while the father and mother, with little five-year-old Charlie, went to visit the mines. Mr. McComas expressed reluctance about going, as the Indians were out on some religious incantation, and were going a peculiar round, and, when they espied a white man, expected to kill or be killed. This was about the state of affairs when these people were caught.

CHAPTER XVIII.

An Active Boy.

A boy at Longmont, Colo., Mrs. Churchill considers one of the wonders of the world in the way of unpremeditated mischief and activity. She asked the landlady for the key to the musical instrument; the woman said she would be obliged to bide her time until she found the key, as it had to be hidden from the active boy. At length the key was produced, but before Mrs. Churchill got the instrument open the boy had the stool unscrewed entirely; while the seat was being adjusted the boy was climbing up on the organ and had seated himself upon an arrangement made to hold a light for the performer, with his bare feet upon the keys as far as he could place them from his position. The boy was routed; the next seen of him he was trying to rig up something with which to hold a hanging lamp in imitation of one in the dining room; he had crooked a wire in a good imitation of his model, but the apparatus for holding the lamp was not at hand; the fellow was patiently trying

the room was so located that the patient would
have been obliged to dress herself entire to in-
form upon the little busybody. He wanted to
see her around; said it made him lonesome to
know that she was in the house and not to be
seen. The day he had been most annoying, a
noise as of running water had been heard in the
adjoining rooms; upon investigation it was found
that a faucet had been turned on to wash a little
wagon and the water left running, because it was
hard to turn, too much for the boy's strength, so
he left it to be discovered by the business men
occupying the rooms below. Mrs. Churchill put
on a colored wrapper and made her way to the
landlady's apartment, just in time to encounter
a business man from below asking with emphasis,
"What was the matter with the pipes above?"
The woman hurried to the sink and found the
little red wagon left, as the owner had fled when
he discovered that he could not turn the faucet
to stop the water. When Mrs. Churchill was
ready to depart, that active boy had managed to
get cleaned up that he might, with his father,
stand at the head of the out-leading stairway and
shake hands and say good-bye, and come and stop
with us when you are up again. There was a

188

The boy's activity was only equalled by his patience. Without any reasonable chance to do a sane and useful thing in the way of development, he would work for hours as if he had been inspired from some unseen source. It would be interesting to know how he put in his time when spending the summer with his grandmother on the farm. How could he be kept from diving in the first deep water hole he found is a mystery. The sages tell us that real genuine genius is more the outcome of energy and patience than any other quality. This child is certainly a little abnormal, but probably not more so than others that might be named, who, when mature, astonished the world with wondrous achievements. This boy had all the vanity requisite to great things. There used to be housekeepers with more energy than sense—the everlasting scrubber; the over-neat woman. Since the better education of woman has come to stay this type of woman has disappeared almost, if not entirely. The typical scold has gone the same way, still the law can be found on the statute books from which this country gets her primitive code, that permits a husband to put her on a ducking board if she scolds. All that ailed those poor women was more energy than mental resource. The law of ducking could not work a cure in such a case. Another generation had to come to the rescue and give the woman of energy a chance for expansion. There are of both sexes people who have wasted a vast amount of very valuable talent and energy for want of the development to suit the case. All vegetable and animal life have deformities and blights; God's chosen are no exception to natural law. He may by virtue of being the first or foremost of animal law by opportunity almost reach the dignity of a semi-god, or for lack of development become the chattering imbecile. After all is not the cake of tallow and the hot poker a better imitation of the tin mender's efforts than the usual methods of little folks. Children's play is only imitation of real business life, and the child that makes the best imitation certainly is the most gifted. None of this child's efforts were so bungling as the mud pie manufacturing. Mrs. Churchill made ovens that would bake and chimneys that would draw, and takes a pride in the memory thereof; they were made of red clay and brick and were quite artistic.

CHAPTER XIX.

ACCIDENTS IN COLORADO.

FIRST TRIP TO GEORGETOWN.

The first time Mrs. Churchill was at George-town, Colorado, she had an unpleasant affair, that bore far-reaching effects. It was ten o'clock p. m. when the stage reached the interesting little city. The guests were shown to their rooms, Mrs. Churchill being left to the last; so it was discovered that she was unattended by another. She protested against being left to the last one located. She was put in room fourteen, upstairs, a forbidding looking top floor. At two in the morning a couple of men came to the door, presumably landlord and clerk. As one confirmed what the other said it was known that there were two individuals. They stated that they were railroad men, and "you have our room," they said. "You leave that door instantly or you will have a ball put into your carcass, if not more than one," was the rejoinder. They answered, "Fire away." Mrs. Churchill did not wait for the second invitation, but fired three balls into the door. As there was no thud she concluded the gallant U. S. A. man, woman's protector, had stepped aside at the invitation, and sneaked noiselessly downstairs after hearing the shots. There was no more disturbance that night. In the morning, as soon as the clerk was at the office to get pay unjustly for a night's lodging, Mrs. Churchill took her departure for a private boarding house. Here she told her grievance. Never thinks it her duty to keep a man's secrets for him. This was not her secret. The landlady where she had private board was well protected herself, as she had a vacation college girl rooming with her, besides an immense dog, which laid at her door upon a rug. Besides, she had a big six-shooter, which could be introduced to her legal protectors if things became dangerous. This occurrence was before the great Leadville strike, which resulted in giving it the name of being the greatest silver camp on earth, or Mrs. Churchill would have left for Leadville and taken Georgetown on the return trip. As it was she remained one night longer, taking a great number of subscribers, many of whom took the paper every year during their own lifetime from this period. The second night of her stay the room she occupied was located next to one which

193

opened upon a stairway that led to the street.
This gave the evil disposed a chance to congre-
gate in the room at the head of the stairs, where,
if they could do no worse, could drive a volume
of smoke from cigars into the room that would
smother a woodchuck. The rooms were a suite
of two. There was a door between, well fastened,
as this was a matter never to be neglected by a
lady traveler. At about eleven o'clock the seance
began. Mrs. Churchill knew the only thing to
be done was to draw her bed to the window. As
the bed was a cot this favored the situation, so
that she could lie with head out of the window,
which gave her an opportunity, in spite of the
wicked, to get several hours' sleep. Mrs. Churchill had her way of showing the U. S. A. dude
that he was living in a country that encourages
men in the worst phases of falsehood and hypoc-
risy that the human race can know. The next
day she changed her location, well satisfied with
her list of patrons. The whole matter was written up and published in her paper. She did not
have time to do investigating enough to get
names, or she would at this late date give their
names for the information of posterity. The
landlord keeping the American house at that

time saw Mrs. Churchill six weeks after the episode, and told her that he was obliged in that time to close the house, as the boarders left. The house was never occupied again, although a building of thirty or forty rooms. This tragedy took place in the latter part of the summer of 1879. In 1907 the old American house was taken down and cremated. Such is the fate of tyrants. Most of the animals calling themselves men, who had a hand in the affair, have shared the same fate, only they may not have been cremated on this side, as they were wanted for a crematory already established since some time during the decline of the Roman Empire. Mrs. Churchill went every year to Georgetown, notwithstanding the revelation, proving the courage of her convictions that women have the same right to the business world that men have, and that she has a right to an existence without making a commercial transaction with a sacred reservation. Men have given us our moral code, and assume to be the guardians of virtue. They must either make good some pretences, or come across a Carrie Nation now and then, who will enforce laws in the only manner in which women can enforce them.

CHAPTER XX.

THE BOULDER EPISODE.

Mrs. Churchill was in Boulder county, Colorado, and making her way to the mines above the city. The conveyance was a small mail wagon that would carry about four persons comfortably. The driver's name was Hinman. He had the reputation of being the meanest man in the county. Mrs. Churchill said, "If this is a fact how come he by a federal position?" Most likely has to give bonds for a place of so much responsibility. It being a cold, bleak route, with no great financial inducement, no one cared to take the route, so it was let to the meanest man in the county. If he perished no one cared. It is supposed that even the man himself did not care, as was subsequently proven. Going up to the settlement he made some proposition to Mrs. Churchill that she did not answer, as Solomon says, "Answer not a fool according to his follies." Mrs. Churchill told him at what place she wished to stop, as with those people she was acquainted. When the stage drove up to the door a matron came out and greeted the lady occupant, and further remarked: "We are going to have a lyceum meeting to-night, and as an attraction would be glad to have you speak for us on your favorite topic." Mrs. Churchill is not of sufficient physical vigor to make a business of speech making and attending to the money-making department of running a paper at the same time. In some of the mining camps there is a dearth of amusements and almost anything is acceptable. Mrs. Churchill made the speech and met with her usual success. The next day she was returning to the city of Boulder, when within a few rods of the train she was to take the wagon rolled off a bridge that was not protected by stringers. Mrs. Churchill fell backwards about thirteen feet, striking first upon the top of her head. A high-crowned hat saved her neck from being broken. The man had taken a bolt from the tongue of the wagon, so that the tongue lost control of the vehicle. He knew just when to get out of the stage himself, and managed the affair so much to his advantage that not a strap of his was injured. The hind wheels were only over the edge of the bridge far enough to throw out his only passenger. Women who were camping

article, stating the particulars and the revenge. This was published in her own paper and read extensively in that county. It some way came about that the fellow lost his job as mail carrier, his family cast him off, and he seemed to lose all power to save himself from becoming a wandering vagabond. The tragedy occurred in the latter part of summer. That winter he redeemed himself by committing suicide. The community where he lived felt a sense of relief when he was out of the way. Verily, "the way of the transgressor is hard."

The great heart of the people like to see fair play, whether they are willing to put themselves out to get it or not.

CHAPTER XXI.

GOING DRIVING—A SONG.

Bring up Nancy, brush her coat off, she likes to
have us so.

Get the harness, put it on her, do the best you
know;

Take the whip out, do not touch her—this is just
for show.

Nancy takes us o'er the prairie, through the dust
and snow,

To the distant farm house where we wish to go.

While we gossip, Nancy listens for a friend or
foe,

First with one ear, then the other, until we are
ready to go;

Then she puts her ears straight forward, as if to
show the way,

And we know that she is thinking of her home,
her oats and hay.

appearance of being closely connected to his Satanic Majesty. One could hardly conceive of anything that could be done to make a meaner looking creature made in the image of his Creator. An expressman brought the horse to the South Carolina girl and Mrs. Churchill, a circumstance of which they should have been very suspicious, but when they learned the place he was dealing with, it was too late. The people who had that corral had the reputation of picking up the women's horses that were pasturing on the common, putting them in the corral and selling them to country buyers. It would not pay for a man to leave his business and hunt the horse, as the country had an immense range for market. Bringing them to justice by any of the then existing legal processes would have called for the output of a gold mine. Few people have ever been able to protect themselves by legal methods in this country of the people, by the people and for the people. The horse was found to be perfectly fearless of anything in a railroad centre; was handsome and gentle to handle, but had the runaway habit established before she was sold to this printing establishment. Two of the printer young ladies were taking off the harness, when she conceived the idea that as she had lost the opportunity while being driven, she would avail herself of that privilege while being unharnessed. This for horse wickedness was without a parallel in the experience of those office incumbents. Mrs. Churchill was the next one to be victimized by the runaway habit and was picked up unconscious, the buggy strung all over the country. After Mrs. Churchill's recovery she went out on a canvassing trip and was gone a month. Upon her return she learned of the remarkable exploits of this piece of horse flesh. The South Carolina printer girl, who was an expert horsewoman, was the next victim, being obliged to keep her bed for three weeks and hire her printing done. She would not permit any one to notify Mrs. Churchill of what had taken place, for fear Mrs. Churchill would come home, as the bills of the establishment had begun to fail of payment because of the loss of time on account of these accidents. On Mrs. Churchill's return the matter was talked over, and a conclusion reached that the only thing to be done was to sell the "naughty beast" that did not know enough to appreciate being a printers' pet. She was sold at a reduced price, but as both parties had suffered about in equal pro-

upsetting. This incident had the further effect of confirming the mascot business. The train had an emigrant car, which was turned upon the side, the window broken, so that the snow and mud from the snow sheds, the accumulation of years, came upon the unfortunate, terror-stricken occupants. One at a time they cleared themselves as far as possible of the appearances of disaster, and came into the upright coach. There were among the victims a man and wife, the man a giant in stature and size, the woman an average sized female. They were Swedes, but spoke English very well, were comfortably dressed and respectable in appearance. The woman was sobbing when they came in the upright coach. Said she through her sobs, "They always put the emigrant coach in the very worst place." The husband had a scalp wound, neither knew how serious it might be, and both were suffering, as all the passengers were, from the strain of a terrible fright. The couple seated themselves and the woman began combing the man's hair in order to get the clay and dirt out, so as to know how badly he might be injured. It was soon known that his scalp wound was not at all serious, and the couple became calm, pursuing the work of clearing their heads of dirt. After the man had been made presentable he arose to his feet, unbraided the woman's long strands of very dark brown hair, combed and brushed them with as much delicate tact as if he were a professional ladies' hairdresser. His immense size seemed to have the effect of making the scene a particularly pathetic one. There was a tenderness displayed while restoring the braids with those immense fingers that left few dry eyes that witnessed this scene. These accidents all came about the same year. It seems as if the world was put up on a trouble plane. If one is having anything like fair sailing weather some one will "sit up and take notice," and if it is possible, spring a trouble trap of one nature if not another. Mrs. Churchill was once at Cripple Creek. She had got through the place and its abounding suburbs. The expressmen were sought; one was engaged, promising to be on time at the required hour. It occurred to Mrs. Churchill that she had seen that face before, and that he gave her an amused, quizzical look. The time came, but no expressman. All at once her wits were sharpened, she remembered the fellow; that he had been employed to do the express work on the paper at Denver and

CHAPTER XXIV.

A Retreating Campaign.

When Mrs. Churchill first came to Denver it was expected that she would call upon the leading women and get their permission to publish a Woman's Right paper, show her credentials and so forth, join some association, so as to be in a position to be brought to time, if audacious enough to criticise the established customs, or to do anything really original. Mrs. Churchill remained in Denver long enough to know that the climate was just what she needed; the rest might, with properly directed energy, be forthcoming. For several years she had been traveling; and a person conducting a retreating campaign would not be likely to have many acquaintances who could give letters to strangers as to her worth. There was a humiliation in the very idea that such a course was necessary. She came, she saw and conquered. No doubt it was not exactly the best thing she could have done, but she had in memory a time when a man was permitted to introduce her to an audience. It seemed to make jealousies. It seemed to her as if every man in the audience thought he owned the speaker, and was the only owner. It was the last time any man ever had the opportunity. If Mrs. Churchill had presented herself in her working apparel to even the leading suffragists of Denver no explanation would have been equal to a personal appearance, above reproach. Mrs. Churchill is naturally defective in style; has a mind which runs upon other things. This is no crime, nor is it a crime for a woman or a man to like a fine personal appearance. Cruel, foolish criticism is where the crime is to be found.

A WOMAN'S CONVENTION.

The original Woman's Suffrage society was very much in debt. It had been badly managed, and had not been doing any effectual work for a couple or three years. In 1876 this society had probably done its very best, as the question was voted upon that year, as the territory was admitted to statehood at that time. The result was a losing one by six thousand majority. The Mexican element are accredited with this failure. It would not be a matter of surprise after this outcome if the society should become somewhat apathetic. Mrs. Churchill, with the help of some of the women from outside towns, called a convention. The city women, perhaps troubled because of their laurels, came in and were at once installed in the offices, thus giving experienced people a chance to at least make themselves useful as well as ornamental. Mrs. Churchill steadfastly refused office, as the conducting of a paper in the interests of the cause was enough for any one head.

The convention adjourned with the best of feeling. The men's papers made all the capital they possibly could out of the fact that Mrs. Churchill was not given office, assuming that the honor of such a position would have been irresistible to any mortal woman with healthy ambition. Mrs. Churchill seems to have been created superior to such a thing as personal aggrandizement. What she wants is a civilization that will come somewhere near filling the wants of the great mass of the people. Federal control of schools; that general illiteracy from any cause may disappear from the world. The idea of holding children responsible for the bad management of those interested in ignorance and depravity, and those gone before, is repugnant to any fair-minded person. If women could be induced to perform their public duties, which would be to become a helpmeet for man in public affairs as in private matters, many things could be done that are now wholly neglected. The minds of such men as Chaucer and Ruskin have given this subject attention and have concluded that man will only cease being a marauder and a warrior when women do enough to teach them that there is nothing in the course usually pursued by the masculine portion of the human family. We now have rapid transportation, which will furnish sufficient opportunity for crossing races without resorting to war, which simply means death to the other male and additional number of female slaves in the market.

DEVELOPMENT OF WOMAN SUFFRAGE IN COLORADO.

In 1893 the Populist party came into power in the state of Colorado. This is the party that voted on woman's citizenship and gave her a majority vote of six thousand. Mrs. Churchill's papers had been published for the period of fourteen years. During these years Idaho's legislature granted woman citizenship, and the right of a citizen was bestowed upon the women of Utah by a constitutional provision. Mrs. Churchill's papers were extensively read in all those localities. Women should be in the councils of every municipality in the United States. Men do not know all there is to be known and put into execution for the welfare of the race. Women can be educated to fill positions with a fearless care for right, ignoring the personal ambition phase of the position. When we have a higher standard of general intelligence this is what will likely come to pass.

Mrs. Churchill was never popular with the W. C. T. U., because popularity was not what she was looking for. A better condition of things was her watchword. Her methods were her own. She never tried to persecute any organization, or belittle them, because their methods were different from her own. One of the Anthony family, living at Leavenworth, Kas., once wrote to have Mrs. Churchill get interested in his business. Mrs. Churchill was fairly harassed by these importunities from different sources, and answered these letters rather saucily sometimes. Susan B. Anthony perhaps realized that there was younger blood in the field and may have thought her laurels in danger. When the brother failed to

interest the new woman in his schemes, she had
no further use for Mrs. Churchill and would show
her resentment as opportunity made it possible.
Lucy Stone exchanged papers with Mrs. Churchill
for fourteen years, but in all that time never had
a good word for Mrs. Churchill or her work.
Mrs. Churchill thought the question for which
she was giving her life work of more importance
than self-aggrandizement. It has ever seemed to
her most queer that women or men either could
be so easily set up and so much more in love
with themselves than the cause they represent.
Society in general do not like originality, especially in woman, as it looks like defying man's
authority for a woman to prefer her own methods
to accepting those laid down for the majority.
Ministers have been known to ridicule women
from their pulpits because all went jumping over
the fence with the crowd and even keeping up the
imitating process after the bar had been removed. Men have ever been a guilty quantity
for ridiculing women for being whatever men desired them to be and had striven to make them.
The story of the poor colored people, who wonder
why they are made the subject of belittling
jokes is appropriate here. What have they ever

done to make us superior to jumping over the same fence, even after the last rail is removed. Woman has been systematically educated to spend her conversational ability upon the most frivolous topics. This has the effect to belittle her range of thought so that she can comprehend only superficialities. The popular colleges of the United States are turning out more educated people with less originality and fewer geniuses than any other country.

LICENSED ROWDYISM.

It is difficult to explain why college boys and girls should be upheld in displaying the most flagrant rowdyism. Any other class of the community who were disturbing the peace of the community in a similar manner would be called to order by the police force if there were no other methods. This may be a popular phase of defiant vanity; if so, it is vulgar enough to meet with explanation of motive and the reproof of authority.

CHAPTER XXV.

THE SONG OF "SARAH JANE" HEN.

I had a lovely dappled hen,
  I could not trace her stock,
But by the speckles in her dress
  Should think her Plymouth Rock.

Be what she may in ancestry,
  It would be hard to find again
Hen with so many winning ways,
  We call her Sarah Jane.

She meets me at the garden gate
  In sunshine and in rain,
To ask about the kind of scraps
  I have for Sarah Jane.

This is the only hen around
  That looks to chances main;
This diplomatic turn of mind
  Belongs to Sarah Jane.

THE SONG OF "SARAH JANE" HEN.

When sick and almost unto death
   She sang her old refrain;
When held for a dose of kerosene
   My patient Sarah Jane.

Her comb is pale, her eyes are dim,
   But still she takes her grain.
I'll try to keep my courage up
   In hope for Sarah Jane.

If I should chance to lose this hen,
   Should feel that life is vain,
As far as chickens are concerned,
   So much for Sarah Jane.

LATER.

My hen has passed from life to death,
   From affection, joy or pain,
But Martin Farquer Tupper
   Gives me hopes for Sarah Jane.

In his philosophy he says
   If man shall rise again
His dog is entitled to this life,
   Then why not Sarah Jane.

217

ACTIVE FOOTSTEPS.

The pathos of the thing is this:
  She sang her old refrain,
From weakness she could scarcely stand,
  My lovely Sarah Jane.

And when I am dead and gone to heaven
  To walk the golden plane
I am sure I would like to meet this pet,
  My singing Sarah Jane.

I laid her body in the earth,
  But upon the cheek a stain
Proved plainly that a tear had dropped
  In love for Sarah Jane.

CHAPTER XXVI.

THE SOAPWEED MAN.

A SONG.

His beard may glow with sunlight,
   His eyes reflect the blue,
Hair like the tangled soapweed,
   Toes coming through his shoes.

He will eat upon the doorstep
   Of one who gives her mite,
And it never once to him occurs,
   But that this act is white.

This man sprang from the soapweed,
   While the Indian, in his lair,
May have come from Ursa Major,
   Or the little black tamarack bear.

The two are men for a' that,
   Their right must in the main
Be dear to every mother,
   Though they sleep upon the plain.

Despise, then, not thy brother,
   Although a soapweed man,
For is not the very soapweed
   A part of the heavenly plan?

CHAPTER XXVII.

THE DIFFERENCE.
A SONG.

Woman sings the lullaby,
Man the serenade;
Man writes the music for the race
And wears the gay cockade.

For virtues that are quiet,
Woman holds the sway;
For noise, for strife, for riot,
Great man should keep the day.

The two it takes to make a whole
In nature's wondrous plan,
And counsel without a woman's soul
Proves the poorest works of man.

Thus all nature's difference
Proves all nature's tact,
And shallow is the mental grade
That denies this natural fact.

CHAPTER XXVIII.

A Trip Up the Red River.

Mrs. Churchill was in New Orleans and wanted to go up the river to Shreveport, from thence to Texas. The first thing to be done was to find a captain of a river boat who was a gentleman. This came about satisfactorily; the captain proved to be worthy the name in every respect. There were several gentlemen on board who had been to New Orleans and were returning home. All were sociable and very agreeable. Mrs. Churchill had a new Moody and Sankey song book and was singing the familiar old tunes with any lady who could sing with her. The crew were colored men, and musicians, forming a band, whenever there was a call for music. Sabbath day was to be spent on the boat. The gentlemen planters suggested that Mrs. Churchill give a discourse upon the subject of woman's condition as a person not having the power to legislate in her own defense, or in that of hers of either sex. Mrs. Churchill happened to have with her the celebrated discourse delivered by the Rev. Samuel

May some time in the early forties, at Rochester, N. Y. This sermon was printed and extensively circulated, much of the information therein taking root and bearing fruit for a better state of things for the women of the U. S. of A. Mrs. Churchill consented, and in casting about for something resembling a pulpit on deck consulted an intelligent colored man, one of the boat's crew, who proved equal to the emergency. Sabbath morning, just before time for the service, a pile of sieves were placed one upon another until the required height was reached, then a cake board brought and laid across the top sieve and a white towel obscured the top entirely. To use a popular phrase, "this was all right." The sieves were of the variety used by farmers in winnowing grain. Perhaps by this time obsolete; at that time in course of transportation for the farmers' needs. Big, heavy dining room chairs were brought and placed in a ring around the neat little deck. There were about a dozen in their seats. The thirteenth was a big Louisianian, who cared nothing for the subject to be treated, but had a prejudice against women in so public a place as the pulpit of whatever it might be constructed. This man was not very tall but would weigh over two hundred pounds, and had a large swelling on the front of his neck, a chronic disease of the glands. Mrs. Churchill noticed that the seat placed for him was vacant. He stood near but looked out over the water, evidently interested in the scenery, but intending to hear everything said while giving vent to his prejudices at the same time. "Killing two birds with a stone." Mrs. Churchill well understood the gentle nature of the Southern man, so walked up to this stubborn sheep, took him by the arm and said in a sweet, low voice, "Brother, come and sit with us, please; here is a seat prepared for you before the foundations of the earth were laid." He smiled, had been smiling since first approached. Slowly he came, but obediently took the vacant chair and respectfully listened. The sermon was well delivered, as Mrs. Churchill is a born reader, and her voice finely cultivated for reading. The band helped with the music, and the entertainment lasting a little over an hour was pronounced a success. After dinner the gentlemen amused themselves shooting alligators that lay like logs of wood along the banks of the river. At length Shreveport was reached. The planks were placed, people were leaving the boat. The

CHAPTER XXIX.

ODE TO THE FLEETNESS OF THE SUMMER MONTHS.

Oh, Summer Months! why off so soon?
  The storms do beat, the boughs do sigh,
In dread of autumn's chilling moan
  And winter's dreary sky.

Oh, Summer Months! thou didst in haste
  The honeymoon forswear,
And leave us to the wint'ry waste
  Of frosty, biting air.

Oh, Summer Months! how couldst
  To other lands repair,
And leave a child but three months old
  In winter's high-armed chair.

Oh, Summer Months! have you no "hart"
  That panteth after brooks?
Which now are frozen solid ice,
  You might liquidate with looks.

Oh, Summer Months! but what is the use
  Of finding fault with Fate;
You had to leave us when you did,
  Or for others be too late.

CHAPTER XXX.

PLAINT OF THE REJECTED MIRROR.

Must I ever stand in this vacant hall
    And reflect the shadows that pass,
Because my frame is a span too tall
    For the niche for the parlor glass?

My proportions are fine "to perfection;"
    My frame is of maple that curls;
I am faithful in every reflection
    Of fair guests—or serving girls!

And it is hard to be thus rejected
    From the place where I rightly belong;
To stand in the hall so neglected,
    And the time seems so weary and long.

We e'er please the youthful and fair;
    We undeceive plain folks and old;
And of censure receive we our share,
    As the facts we so plainly unfold.

I certainly have a mission,
    A story of truth to be told;
Then move me from a useless position,
    Though a slave in the mart to be sold!

226

For better a slave that is doing,
   Receiving and giving again,
Than to stand here no mission pursuing,
   Merely seen and admired of men.

———

TEXAS.

What in Texas most doth vex us
Is the broken pane;
Death may come in at a window
When there is nothing nigh to hinder,
Even through a broken pane.

CHAPTER XXXI.

THE CLOTHES PIN WORLD.

In a lot of fifty clothes pins,
Suspended from a nail,
A pretty little pinkish pin
Did her fate bewail.

There chanced to be a reddish stripe
A-running through the wood
Of which the fiftieth pin was made,
So she blushed beneath her hood.

There is music in the clothes pins
When they are made to rattle.
The pinkish pin talked on the same;
It may have been but prattle.

"If a clothes pin should aspire
To a telegraphic wire,
Or any higher line,
There is a rumpus
In the basket,
And every one would ask it
For an explanation
To the other forty-nine."

THE CLOTHES PIN WORLD.

A rusty old pin, nearly split in two,
  Gave as his opinion:
"This will never do.
  This little pinkish pin,
    That is underneath a hood,
  Forgets that her heart
    Is only made of wood;
  That such a burning desire
  To reach something higher
    Might be the means
  Of setting things on fire."

    He continues:
"Who would not be a clothes pin
    And sit upon a line,
  With the same size of head
  And exactly the spread
    Of the other forty-nine?
    No, forty-eight;
  I would be a clothes pin,
    With a path I can define,
  And hold down the fluttering things
    That are placed upon a line,
  With arms securely pinioned.
    (One would think a sorry plight.)
  Not so; we do not hold the lines,
    And our feet are out of sight."

At length the fiftieth clothes pin said
　To the other clothes pins fair:
"The higher up we get
　The better is the air."

　　Continues, grumbling:
"If, when dancing on the line,
　One should chance to stand awry,
One must explain to forty-nine,
　Or they pine away and die.

"It may be a button or a seam,
　Or any other cause,
That would throw a figure out of line,
　And the clothes pin world will pause.

"While the wry is cogitating
　In her little wooden head,
The cruel winds come howling down
　And try her powers of spread.
What the cyclone fails to do
　May a careless hand complete,
And a clothes pin, split in two,
　Is lying at our feet."

And forty-nine stand on the line,
　All trembling in surprise

THE CLOTHES PIN WORLD.

That one within the clothes pin world
　　Should so aspire to rise.

Fifty clothes pins were in a basket sprawled.
　　They squirmed and rattled into place
Until a halt was called.
　　The hair would have been worn from Pinkey,
But she was already bald.

A hand appeared upon the scene
　　And took the basket down.
The fiftieth pin was chosen
　　To wear a hood and gown.

Because of her pink complexion
　　This pin received a call
To take a place among the toys
　　That grace a parlor wall.

The rest were much disgruntled,
　　But continued on their way,
To play and dance upon the line
　　With every washing day.

CHAPTER XXXII.

STRAWBERRYING.

(Copied from "Over the Purple Hills.")

The queen of all berries seems to be fraught with misfortune for me; perhaps it would have been different had I been a June bird, instead of a snow bird; the frosty, dark December being my natal month. Be that as it may, I have had a serious experience in my efforts to obtain strawberries all through life, and the evil genius continues to pursue me, as it does some persons in love matters. When a child I remember being in a meadow in quest of the small variety of wild fruit, and after filling my basket and starting for home, of missing my calculations and falling backwards into a deep-seated, contemptibly narrow little rivulet. My berries were upset in the water and lost, and I went home in a frightful plight, and to crown my distress some distinguished little people were waiting to see me. The inconvenience of making a presentable toilet with the amount of skulking to be done under the circumstances was something fearful to undergo at the time, and painful to contemplate even at this distant day.

Upon another occasion, not having the fear of man nor his laws before my eyes, I trespassed upon the property of a hermit bachelor. This wretched old fossil was the terror of the village, especially among women and children; and this act of mine goes far towards proving a disposition prone to daring adventure, if not foolhardiness, in early life, for there was not a grown woman in the neighborhood who would have ventured to cross his estate, and I should never have thought of looking for berries upon the giant's causeway if it had not been at his own suggestion. The old fellow met a flock of children in the lane and took it upon himself to threaten any one who should go into his fields in search of strawberries. I thought the matter over, and came to the conclusion that there must be something in those meads worth looking after, or the man would not have taken so much pains as to threaten the children that were in ignorance of the fact. I procured a basket and stole away, reached the forbidden ground and filled the little receptacle, which held about a quart. The everlasting pink sunbonnet which was worn in those days so obscured my sight or range of vision that the crazy old barbarian might have alighted upon me at any time and carried me off to his dark, dismal bachelor's den, all covered with blood and bones, and there he might have buried your humble servant, basket and all, beneath the rickety floor, and no one would have known but a black bear had carried her off, as they were in the habit of doing with wicked children in olden times. The old fellow was on hand in time to spoil my picnic, however, although perhaps he had no idea of becoming the chief actor in an infant tragedy. Well, when I was ready to go home, and in fact in the act of scaling the stake and rider fence, the giant came and caught me by the foot. The bothering sunbonnet was to blame for all this. I might have escaped without this encounter had there been a fair range of vision. He brought me to the ground, took my basket of berries and poured them into his smoky old hat, and then tried his best to make his little black dog bite me. The dog was a harmless, stupid cur, and was so delighted to see a child upon the premises that he wagged his tail and looked pleased in spite of the dreadful situation. The old man had been watching, likely, from the time I came into the field, and had kept the dog in the house, having made up his mind to confiscate the contraband fruit;

234

if the dog barked it would be likely to interfere
with his plans. I was frightened nearly to death,
and climbed the fence in the greatest possible
haste, holding the empty basket upon my arm.
I had no apologies to make, only threatened the
hermit with my two big half brothers, who would
have thrashed him within an inch of his life had
they ever known anything of the affair. It would
not have mattered about the trespass; the berries
were wild and not considered as sacred as if he
had planted and hoed them; besides, my kind-
hearted brothers did not give the man the credit
for having sufficient poetry in his soul to appreciate a strawberry patch, and his uncalled for
threats in the lane were enough to arouse the
curiosity of any enterprising youth. I know now
that my brothers were such treasures as rarely
fall to the lot of the second family of children, and I worshiped them both as towers of
strength and masculine tenderness; and for fear
of getting them in trouble that might end by having them go to jail (the terror of an unsophisticated child), with the instinct of a woman, I
never told of my adventure with the hermit
bachelor. The old fellow comprehended the situation and knew about how to manage the affair.

The loss of the berries was a small item in this adventure; getting away alive was the important part. Upon another occasion, and while still a youth, I had been appointed teacher for a class in Sabbath school, and when returning from devotional service one Sunday afternoon in the balmy month of June, planned an excursion with one of my pupils—by the way, a girl taller than myself,—and of course she should have known better, but neither of us had the grace to withstand the green fields, the fragrant air and the ripening strawberry patch. She, poor girl, child like, went in full dress; my wardrobe was never very elaborate, owing to constitutional indifference to such things. We tarried late, got wet by a passing shower, she lost a valuable piece of jewelry, and both were severely reprimanded for our losses and desecration of the Sabbath; so much for the forbidden fruit. Perhaps it was strawberries that Eve divided with Adam; I should not wonder. I went strawberrying in the great Yosemite valley; the same evil genius followed; the effort made me very ill; unsympathizing tourists devoured my hard-earned fruit, when I was too sick to look after worldly matters; and this brings us down to the present period, as a

Second Advent preacher would say. Not long
since, a woman living in the town of Greeley
(that place is peculiar for feminine assertion)
sent me a basket of strawberries, at the same time
addressed me a note stating all the particulars,
and how I should proceed to fill my part in the
program; go to the express office at such an hour.
The day dragged slowly away; I wrote strawberries on half a dozen pieces of blank paper lying
about the office, and thought of nothing else for
the whole day; at seven o'clock I chased off to all
the express offices in town, going to the wrong
ones first, and the right one last, but to learn that
the train was late. I was not so sure but that
I was early. A friend came in at evening, and
I related the story of my prospects and he volun-
teered to look up the berries if they were in town;
he went and was told that nothing was delivered
from this office after seven o'clock p. m. He returned and reported, but promised to attend to it
by seven next morning. I waited in fearful suspense; the berries were now twenty-four hours
picked, were considered perishable, and what was
best of all, were a tribute of esteem from an indulgent friend, and I felt more anxious than the
value of the berries from a sordid standpoint

or it would have been delivered; that in all probability my friend had failed in getting them shipped as she expected. I gave them up again, but in the course of the morning found myself at the depot where the express matter is first placed after being unloaded from the cars; was there informed the same; no such package. At last, and as I was about to give it up for the third time, an employe said he had an idea that he had a vague recollection that there was a package of this kind sent out in the wagon a few moments before. I thought perhaps they would reach my office by the time I reached it at noon; sure enough, they came, first to the office of my friend, who had been out doing his level best for that two quarts of berries, and true to his trust had brought them to my office. But the end is not yet: I came home, hulled the berries, gave my friend a dish, and prepared some with sugar for myself. Just then a bore came in, and as I had to write a letter acknowledging the berries before the next mail went out, it was three o'clock before I was at liberty to taste those precious berries; by this time I had suffered twenty-four hours' dreadful suspense, undergone unusual physical exertion, and the berries were thirty-six hours old.

239

a pair of cloth gaiters with rubbers at the side
(obsolete now), and with her lighted lantern has-
tened to the wood pile, secured an axe and made
her way to the bridge, not however, without slip-
ping a couple of times, as the path leading down
the hill to the bridge lay in a bed of clay, when wet
about as slippery as anything could well be. The
distressed party could, from his position, see that
preparations were being made for his relief, and
waited in breathless anxiety. When the bridge
was reached she found a man there holding a
horse by the bit. The animal's hind feet were
fettered between a couple of planks, loosened and
raised by the water, yet bound by a couple of
wooden pins, which held them to the stringers.
Mrs. Churchill took the bit while the man pried
up the plank and released the horse, so that he
could regain his footing. If the man had gone ten
feet further he and his horse must both have been
lost, as the other end of the bridge had gone out,
and the current was very powerful. The accident
was all that saved both man and beast. The person in trouble spoke little English and that was
very broken. Mrs. Churchill led the way to her
home and showed the man where a comfortable
stable would shelter the horse, a diminutive little

the night before that it would have been quite
impossible to sleep in them. Before going to
bed he had been furnished with dry clothing.
He had donned his own apparel and shown
sufficient intelligence to place them near the
big stove to dry. He took breakfast and
without a word disappeared, leaving the little
"beasties" to the great delight of the children,
who did not care much if the silent man should
not return. He came again at the expiration of
three months and took the little mother, but left
the colt, likely for expenses. Mrs. Churchill
says now that she thinks the silent man may
have been a halfbreed Indian, as they are the
most silent people known, and very sensitive
about many things. The mother mare was Canadian and Shetland stock. The colt had an
Arabian strain and was very interesting. It was
fed, petted and curried until it was three years
old, then found its way into a show company.
The Indian wars scattered the settlement and
made it necessary to dispose of everything but
a scanty wardrobe and leave the country for
more peaceful parts.

CHAPTER XXXIV.

MONTE DIABLO.
(Copied from "Over the Purple Hills.")

Monte Diablo is the name of a prominence three thousand eight hundred and fifty-eight feet above the level of the sea. This point occurs about twenty-eight miles from San Francisco, and is the terminus of one spur of the coast range. There are many higher points upon the coast than Monte Diablo, but from its peculiar position it gives one of the most extensive landscape views in the known world. The eye has a range from Lassen's Peak in the north to Whitney's in the south, a distance of three hundred and twenty-five miles, giving an area as large as the whole state of New York. The Farallone Islands, forty miles out at sea, can be traced rising in the misty distance like the white walls of a vast storehouse. The checkered streets of San Francisco with its shipping may be seen upon one hand and the dome of the State House at Sacramento upon the other. In the north looms up the weird Buttes and the snow clad Shasta, and in the east the cloud capped Sierras. Thirty-six

creatures. In fact, the cañon seemed a thoroughfare where the fog was drafted by the air
from the ocean and valley to certain points near
the mountain tops. The course of these flying
vapors was so marked, and they flitted so steadily
but silently by, that they formed a feature of
great interest. The doors of the hotel had been
closed to prevent any straggling damps from
entering; everything appeared foggy and gloomy.
All at once a west window was lighted up, as if
by the sudden blaze of a bonfire. A young girl
screamed and looked frightened, exclaiming "O
dear, the valley is all on fire!" As the sun was
sinking in the west and his beams assumed the
right focus, all this gloom changed in the twink-
ling of an eye, and the fog became a bright flame
color, still keeping its billowy identity. View-
ing it from the elevation of the hotel some distance above the valley the effect was wonderful.
In a few moments it changed from a flame color
to a light yellow, and as the sun disappeared it
shed a beautiful pink shade upon the mist, giving
the ravine and whole valley the appearance of
being draped in undulating folds of pink tarlton.
This gradually faded to white, then to a leaden
blue, and the last that I saw of the scene, those

misty ghosts were chasing one another up the ravine, just as they did before the illumination, only a little faster and with vapors more condensed.

The next morning I ascended the summit that I might see what had become of those foggy flocks driving for the hill tops the night before. There they were to my astonishment; having reached a certain altitude they had halted to rest, hovering over the foot-hills upon the south side of Monte Diablo, completely covering them from sight, like so many snowy fleeces, for they had changed the lead colored traveling dress and were all robed in white. The summit of Diablo was entirely above this ocean of mist and upon the north the landscape was as clear as if the hills upon the south side of the point were not entirely enveloped in this downy covering. What a kind provision of nature! the drafts of air suck these clouds of fog up the ravines; here they cling around the hill tops until eaten up by a tropical sun, or are poured out in draughts of rain, which runs into the valleys, giving this water first to the mountains, next to the valleys, lastly the rivers. Truly,

"He moves in a mysterious way,
His wonders to perform."

At this season of the year the clouds do not
amount to rain, although they moisten vegeta-
tion wherever they appear, that is, all along the
coast, and save the necessity of irrigation.

Old Sol in his morning rounds searches out
every obscure hollow or indentation where
vapors had dared to gather during his tempor-
ary absence, and when his beams strike the spot
little spirits of vapor are seen to rise up as dis-
tinctly and rapidly as the smoke from the flue
of a chimney and are gone in a moment, swal-
lowed by this yellow-faced ogre. Looking down
upon this ocean of fog, I could imagine it peopled with ethereal beings, as it would require
but an occasional flap of angel wings to keep
afloat upon this beautiful sea of glory.

When sinking nearly through, one could
obtain a rare view of the scarlet poppy fields,
the soft green hills and picturesque animal life
peacefully grazing, and while the sun is scattering the fog-cloud, I look to the north and see
the discolored waters of the Sacramento and the
San Joaquin rivers wth their soiled tributaries
slowly coursing along, uniting in one body before

passing the Golden Gate to enter the great peaceful ocean. Tracing these rivers from their source until they reach their destiny, how much they resemble the course of human life! Falling from the clouds a pure snow-flake, pillowed for a time upon the lofty mountain tops, there to be warmed into liquid bodies, carried below by circumstances to the great world of usefulness, for a time maintaining its purity of color to the admiration of the sentimental tourist and practical native, dispensing blessings to thirsty vegetable and animal life. As it descends further, it is concentrated into iron pipes and wooden flumes and dashed with Niagara force into the red clay bank to start from its hiding place the yellow gold dust which it baptizes to a new life of usefulness. Here the die is cast, henceforth, until the sea is reached, must the river which first came to earth a snow-flake, travel through all its life of utility with the stain of soil upon its bosom, and the signs of its uses marked in all its varying phases. The days of its romance are ended, the dashing cascade and coquettish waterfall, its wayward wanderings through groves and woods, its deep and quiet thoughtful moods, its spreading out to hold the plain then shrinking to its banks again,

rise again and become a part of the everlasting hills to share alike in their misty cloud-caps, purple mantles and beautiful dresses of green and autumn brown. The birds seem to catch the inspiration of the scene and remain suspended on fluttering wing, hovering over the enchanted valley.

I returned to the Central Pacific Railroad and practical life by the Sanramoon Valley to Livermore. This route to Monte Diablo is most desirable. The Sanramoon Valley is one of the most productive spots in the whole State and is under fine cultivation. Fields of wheat were standing fence high, green as a meadow, and level as a house floor, and so heavily laden as to tremble in the breeze from their weight. Orchards loaded with fruit; in fact, everything wearing a look of luxuriant prosperity. The soil is dark and rich. Shade trees are planted for miles along the public highway. The meadow lark, and linnet, quail and robin, all were singing "more wheat, big wheat, sweet wheat, we'll eat the wheat."

CHAPTER XXXV.

SKETCHES.

ASSISTING GIFTED GIRLS.

Mrs. Churchill has, in the course of her career, rescued several helpless girls, so that they have been able to do better for themselves than many do with willing parents. In the early '70s, in Sacramento, California, she defeated a bill calculated to relegate all single women who supported themselves to the level of the policeman's will. This was done with a burlesque, which treated the men in exactly the same way that women were being treated. The House and Senate concluded that this was no more than just, so would not vote on one bill unless the other could be voted upon also. This same bill was mooted in Denver, when Mrs. Churchill appeared upon the scene with a package of her bills, and the other disappeared. At Austin, Texas, during the administration of Governor Roberts, Mrs. Churchill had the bill presented and passed that keeps the Police Gazette from being sold upon the news stands. This law has been adopted in several different states and spoken of as a success. Mrs. Churchill's motto has ever been to do the race good, and not evil, all the days of her life. She also says it is the interesting people who are subject to criticism, and those whom we would like to drag to a democratic level.

A REMARKABLE MEMORY.

Mrs. Churchill is endowed with a most remarkable memory for recitation, the ability to commit to memory being very rare. She tells an amusing story of herself when first sent to Sunday school in the U. S. of A. Where she had lived prizes were given children who committed the most verses. Things were different in the U. S. But the child tried her own method as being the best she had at command, and felt greatly aggrieved when she learned that she had overdone the thing. There were lessons to be committed by the class, most of whom were not expected to get over two verses in the new testament. When Mrs. Churchill was called upon to begin at the first verse of the chapter, she only ceased the recitation when it was time to close the school. She was then but thirteen years of age and weighed about sixty-five pounds. She thinks now that the teacher made herself fully as ridiculous by coming the next week to engage the little Canadian as a teacher. When the child heard the proposition made to her grandmother she slipped out and hid herself in a hen house, evidently alarmed, and remained until grandmother called to her to come in.

THE IRISH FAMINE.

About this time, in 1845-'6-'7, the so-called civilized world was shocked with the terrible famine in Ireland, which cost 40,000 lives, on account of the failure of the potato crop. Mrs. Churchill came in contact with the Irish of the United States, and learned more about the dreadful situation than would have been probable under any other circumstances. A great part of the food sent to those people from this country never reached them, or reached them in such an adulterated state as to be unfit to sustain life. Mrs. Churchill's grandmother owned a row of frame tenements that were rented to the best of the laboring class of Irish tenants. It was those tenants who kept her wrought up over the calam-

ness, and had two or three hours at her command before the time to take the train. The inquiry made as to the hour the last meal was taken by the patient, she found enough time had elapsed to make it safe to give the patient a bath. Mrs. Churchill sent for warm water and bathed the woman with her own hands, reserving the feet until she should sit up to have her bed changed, that they might be well soaked in salt and water. The feet were washed and wiped and her hair was combed. The patient was able to clean her own teeth. It was most pathetic to see her perform the task of brushing her own teeth, in her weakness. The landlord was now in sight. Mrs. Churchill requested him to get a pail of boiling water and a mop and sponge the floor entirely. The dust was taken up by draining the mop and swabbing the floor as hot as it was possible. Things dry so quickly in this climate. A roll of new carpet, standing in the hall, was brought in and laid upon the floor, fresh and clean. Every article of bedding was changed, the room swept, and furniture dusted. Her garments were changed for fresh things, and when she was put on the bed she said she had not felt as well since she had been taken sick, but now she knew she was going to get well. A list of articles to be cooked for her to eat and change for every meal for a week were arranged until she would be able to dictate her own diet. Mrs. Churchill saw her several years afterwards, when she was the mother of two children, and she always gave Mrs. Churchill credit for saving her life.

THE ROYAL GORGE.

The Arkansas river is, next to the Missouri, the largest contributory of the Mississippi; is 2,000 miles long, and navigable nine months of the year eight hundred miles from the mouth. It divides the great state from which it takes its name into nearly two equal parts. Almost at the upper end of this interesting water course occurs the wonderful cleft in the rocks known as the Royal Gorge, one of the wonders of Colorado, as well as of the world. This gorge is not far from the beautiful city of the canon, called Canon City, a lovely place for residence and a shipping point for a fertile fruit valley. The sources of the great water courses of the country must ever be matters of interest to the tourist, as well as its distinguished peaks. No one should miss the Royal Gorge when touring in Colorado.

CANON CITY—A POEM.

———

Ah Canon! loveliest little city of the Colorado
plain,
Thy life is agricultural, with slow but steady
gain.
The spring time brings the blossoms forth from
many fruitful trees.
Really the harvest time for swarms of worldly
bees.
Later in the season the currant blushes red,
The cabbage lifts above the plain his green ma-
jestic head.
The ripening grain, the purple vine with a world
of garden truck,
Come in the golden harvest time to sustain the
miners' pluck.
Ah Canon! loveliest little city of the Colorado
plain,
Thy life is agricultural, with slow but steady
gain.

C. N. C.

SIGNAL LIVES:
Autobiographies of American Women

An Arno Press Collection

Antin, Mary. **The Promised Land,** 1969

Atherton, Gertrude Franklin [Horn]. **Adventures of a Novelist,** 1932

Bacon, Albion Fellows. **Beauty for Ashes,** 1914

Bailey, Abigail. **Memoirs of Mrs. Abigail Bailey who had been the Wife of Major Asa Bailey Formerly of Landhoff (N.H.),** 1815

Barr, Amelia E.H. **All The Days of my Life,** 1913

Barton, Clara. **The Story of my Childhood,** 1924

Belmont, Eleanor Robson. **The Fabric of Memory,** 1957

Boyle, Sarah Patton. **The Desegregated Heart,** 1962

Brown, Harriet Connor. **Grandmother Brown's Hundred Years,** 1929

Burnett, Frances Hodgson. **The One I Know Best of All,** 1893

Carson, Mrs. Ann. **The Memoirs of the Celebrated and Beautiful Mrs. Ann Carson, Daughter of an Officer of the U.S. Navy and Wife of Another, Whose Life Terminated in the Philadelphia Prison,** 1838

Churchill, Caroline Nichols. **Active Footsteps,** 1909

Cleghorn, Sarah N. **Threescore,** 1936

[Dall, Caroline H.W.]. **Alongside,** 1900

Daviess, Maria Thompson. **Seven Times Seven,** 1924

Dorr, Rheta Child. **A Woman of Fifty,** 1924

[Dumond], Annie H. Nelles. **The Life of a Book Agent,** 1868

Eaton, [Margaret O'Neale]. **The Autobiography of Peggy Eaton,** 1932

Farrar, Mrs. John [Elizabeth Rotch]. **Recollections of Seventy Years,** 1866

Felton, Rebeca Latimer. **Country Life in Georgia in the Days of my Youth,** 1919

Garden, Mary and Louis Biancolli. **Mary Garden's Story,** 1951

Gildersleeve, Virginia Crocheron. **Many a Good Crusade,** 1954

Gilson, Mary Barnett. **What's Past is Prologue,** 1940

Hurst, Fannie. **Anatomy of Me,** 1958

Jacobs-Bond, Carrie. **The Roads of Melody,** 1927

Jelliffe, Belinda. **For Dear Life,** 1936

Jones, Amanda T. **A Psychic Autobiography,** 1910

Logan, Kate Virginia Cox. **My Confederate Girlhood,** 1932

Longworth, Alice Roosevelt. **Crowded Hours,** 1933

MacDougall, Alice Foote. **The Autobiography of a Business Woman,** 1928

Madeleine. 1919

Meyer, Agnes E. **Out of These Roots,** 1953

Odlum, Hortense. **A Woman's Place,** 1939

Potter, Eliza. **A Hairdresser's Experience in High Life,** 1859

Rinehart, Mary Roberts. **My Story,** 1948

[Ritchie], Anna Cora Mowatt. **Autobiography of an Actress,** 1854

Robinson, Josephine DeMott. **The Circus Lady,** 1925

Roe, Mrs. Elizabeth A. **Recollections of Frontier Life,** 1885

Sanders, Sue. **Our Common Herd,** 1939

Sangster, Margaret E. **An Autobiography,** 1909

Sherwood, M[ary] E[lizabeth]. **An Epistle to Posterity,** 1897

Sigourney, Mrs. L[ydia] H. **Letters of Life,** 1866

Smith, Elizabeth Oakes [Prince]. **Selections from the Autobiography of Elizabeth Oakes Smith,** 1924

[Terhune], Mary V.H. **Marion Harland's Autobiography,** 1910

Terrell, Mary Church. **A Colored Woman in a White World,** 1940

Ueland, Brenda. **Me,** 1939

Van Hoosen, Bertha. **Petticoat Surgeon,** 1947

Vorse, Mary Heaton. **A Footnote to Folly,** 1935

[Ward], Elizabeth Stuart Phelps. **Chapters from a Life,** 1896

Wilcox, Ella Wheeler. **The Worlds and I,** 1896

Wilson, Edith Bolling. **My Memoir,** 1938